Poetry Ireland Review 74

Eagarthóir / Editor **Michael Smith**

© Copyright Poetry Ireland Ltd. 2002

Poetry Ireland Ltd./Éigse Éireann Teo. gratefully acknowledges the assistance of The Arts Council/An Chomhairle Ealaíon, the Arts Council of Northern Ireland, and FÁS.

Patrons of Poetry Ireland/Éigse Éireann

Grogan's Castle Lounge
Joan & Joe McBreen
Dillon Murphy & Co.
Office Of Public Works
Richard Murphy
Occidental Tourist Ltd.
Winding Stair Bookshop
Doirín Meagher
Swan Training Institute

Desmond Windle
Eastern Washington University
Fearon, O'Neill, Rooney
Daig Quinn
Twomey Steo Ltd.
Kevin Connolly
Neville Keery
The Irish-American Poetry Society

Poetry Ireland invites individuals, cultural groups and commercial organisations to become Patrons. Patrons are entitled to reclaim tax at their highest rate for all donations of between €128.00 and €12,700. For more details please contact the Director, at Bermingham Tower, Dublin Castle, Dublin 2, Ireland or phone 01 6714262 or e-mail: management@poetryireland.ie

Poetry Ireland Review is published quarterly by Poetry Ireland Ltd. The Editor enjoys complete autonomy in the choice of material published. The contents of this publication should not be taken to reflect either the views or the policy of the publishers.

ISSN: 0332-2998
ISBN: 1-902121-12-0

Editorial Assistant: Paul Lenehan
Cover Template: Colm Ó Cannain
Typography: Barry Hannigan
Cover Photo: 'Texas Fireplace', courtesy of Jerome Guerra

Printed in Ireland by **ColourBooks Ltd.**, Baldoyle Industrial Estate, Dublin13

Contents Poetry Ireland Review 74

	3	**Editorial**
Tony Curtis	5	Still Life With Books
	6	Currach
Maite Díaz Noval	8	Odalisques
David Butler	9	Play
Louise C. Callaghan	10	Skellig Michael
Celia de Fréine	12	Benchmark
	13	Refugee
	14	There was a soldier
Diane Fahey	15	Upstream
	15	Estuary
Ann Egan	16	A Falcon's View
Paul Grattan	18	Maxim
	19	Descartes at Ibrox
T.F. Griffin	20	After Late Summer Separation
	21	I Wanted to Hear your Voice
Heather Jones	22	The Last Chapter of the Toraíocht: Gráinne mourns Diarmuid
Michael Murphy	23	Passage West
Margaret O'Shea	24	I Stand To The North Of Her Always In Shadow
Maureen Oliphant	26	She is under the weeping willow
William Scammell	27	Heft
	27	Litany
Che Qianzi	28	Souvenirs
Ah Jian	29	Missing the Past is also a Life
Geoffrey Squires	30	*from* 'Untitled Poem'
Robert Welch	35	Crosshaven: Neptune Calms the Sea
Fred Johnston	36	The Black Birds
	37	Folk Song
George Seferis	38	Erotikos Logos
Trevor Joyce	42	Love Songs from a Dead Tongue
Tom Mac Intyre	60	Visiting Hours
	62	The Healer's Daughter
Michael S. Begnal	64	It Gets Dark, the Elements
Yael Globerman	65	She Returns

Karen Alkalay-Gut	65	Metamorphosis
Caitlín Maude	66	An Mháthair
Nuala Ní Chonchúir	66	The Mother
Ciaran Carson	68	The Indian Mutiny
Ann Galvin	72	Inside and Outside
Gerard Smyth	73	Hopkins
	74	Portobello Bridge
Dennis O'Driscoll	75	**Pickings And Choosings**
		Tuma Times Two
David Wheatley	86	Get Orf Moy Laaand!
Alex Davis	89	The Native Strain
Alan Titley	92	The World In Irish
Gerald Dawe	97	AudioLogue
Michael S. Begnal	99	Comhthéacsanna Eile
Paul Durcan	106	Letter from one Young Poet to Another
David Lloyd	110	Chaos Theory
Notes on Contributors	119	
Books Received	123	

Editorial

When I accepted the job as Editor of *PIR*, although I knew from past experience as an editor of a poetry journal how difficult it can be to make judgements of rejection or acceptance of submitted work – and to do this under pressure of time and other commitments – I had no idea of the sheer amount of poetry that is submitted to *Poetry Ireland Review*. I had no idea I would be collecting it from the office by the kilo! Nor had I any idea that so many people in Ireland wanted to write poems. Nor indeed that there were so many people outside Ireland who wanted to have their poems considered for publication in *PIR*. Though I hadn't expected it, all of this can be read as a compliment to the track record of *PIR*, its past poets and editors.

Unfortunately, the reality of this editorial work for *PIR* is that only a tiny percentage of unsolicited poems can be accepted. That means hundreds of rejection slips have to be sent out, no doubt causing a great deal of disappointment. To compound the unpleasantness of this, it is practically impossible for me as Editor to respond to submissions with individual comment or criticism.

The best I can do is read what has been submitted and make my own subjective decision to accept or reject. That I can be 'wrong' in that decision, goes without question, and I have to accept the responsibility of my decision. My function is to edit, to accept or reject, not to give the kind of individual, personal advice or tuition that is provided by Creative Writing Courses.

An editor's job is to select, and rejecting material is, unfortunately, an unavoidable part of that. But I would like to offer here and now and collectively, a little advice to prospective contributors to *PIR*: needless to say, this advice is not intended to be taken dogmatically; it is merely a few things I have learnt from personal experience.

1. Appreciate that an editorial decision on your work is subjective and that your rejected submission can always to sent elsewhere.

2. Understand that the editor has rejected your poem(s), not you or your life.

3. Appreciate that *PIR* is the NATIONAL poetry journal and therefore that your work is in competition with the work of many poets who

have been writing for a long time and have already achieved critical recognition. The good side of this is that it really will count for something to have an appearance in *PIR*.

4. Understand that *PIR*, while open to all, is not the appropriate outlet for 'apprentice' work; there should be other outlets for that.

5. Try to distance yourself personally from what you have written, when it is written, realising that it is now words on a page and that it will be responded to, as simply as that. The editor does not know the existential circumstances of your life.

I hope these few words will at least clear up some misunderstandings, if nothing else.

* * *

The outlets for the publication of poetry, as will be obvious from what I have already written, are severely limited. In the autumn issue of *Thumbscrew* (2001), Nicholas Murray, having surveyed the British poetry publishing scene in detail, concludes an interesting piece as follows:

> So, if you were thinking of getting your first collection of
> poems published I would reccommend a little backpacking
> for the next three years. Come back in 2004 and try again.
> You might be lucky, but I wouldn't count on it.

The British situation described by Murray is much the same one we have here in Ireland.

It's a very negative and depressing conclusion. Is there anything positive to be said? I would certainly not recommend the use of a vanity press, which will only serve to get you a bad name. Instead, enter into cooperation with others who share your own passions in poetry and find themselves in a similar situation. Form a co-operative. Use desktop publishing. Join discussion groups or mailing lists on the Internet. Use the web. Create your own readership, however small it may be. That seems to me the best way forward. Don't moan about cliques: some of the best-known poets have started with very few, and developed with only a few hundred readers. With a group of like-minded people, start your own poetry magazine instead of just complaining that your poems are not being accepted by others. Better to have a couple of dozen readers than a couple of dozen rejection slips.

Michael Smith

Tony Curtis

Still Life With Books

Most mornings I wake early
as if I have somewhere to go,
something to do. I potter
for an hour through books,
papers, photographs.
Then I sit by the window
for the rest of the day.

And if there is rain,
I fish for tears.
And if there is mist,
I sift for ghosts.
And if there is snow,
I chisel for stars.

In between
I pace the room
or watch the gate
for the comfort
of the postman.
How did I end up like this?

A watcher of skies
and fields that run to clouds;
a keeper of stillness,
a moon-face at the window,
a love gone to darkness,
a still life with books.

Tony Curtis

Currach

This is my boat.
I made it
with my own hands.
I took salt
from a bitter wind,
hair from
a horse's mane,
thread from
a woman's blouse.

Three stories
my father told me.
The sideways look
my mother has
when she is
curious and alone.
Her silent prayer.
A few rusty nails
from the kitchen door.

Three views of the island:
one in mist, one in rain,
one rocking in a drunken sea.
No flowers.
My people
had no love of leaves,
they saw boats in trees;
now the boats are gone
and the hills are bare.

At night, I sowed
curses into the oars,
rubbed fish oil
into the wood,
for I knew the journey
that lay ahead.
My people's story
was written on water.
Most of it is washed away.

My grandfather
knew the tale
but he'd not tell it.
His ghost sits
in the stern
saying:
*"The future
is a steady course,
row strongly."*

Maite Díaz Noval

Odalisques
translation of 'Odaliscas' by David Butler

The rose-bed is heavy with rivalries.
Each head the mouthing of concupiscence;
Intimate whites, reds dark as sin,
A pout, then a slow undressing.

There are deadening jealousies abroad;
Languorous perfumes that trap insects
All through the long afternoon. But here
Is the shock of sudden innocence.

Cruellest is the discarding of petals,
The swoon to the earth of the faded;
The jaded glance of the envious who
Cling to the knees of bald stamen.

Odaliscas
La huerta de rosas se llena de celos: / Cada flor es la boca de una sinvergüenza / Que hace pucheros y luego despliega / Blanca de enaguas, carmesí cachondo. / / He aquí unas mortíferas rivalidades / En los perfumes que atrapan zumbidos / A lo largo de la tarde lánguida; mas de repente / He el choque de la inocencia inesperada. / / Lo más cruel es el decaimiento continuo / De las viejitas que desmayan al suelo; / De las marchitas envidiosas que aún se pegan / A las rodillas de sus calvos estambres.

David Butler

Play

'Which role is the greatest?' you ask.

Your eyes move from the Captain,
His sword bare as allegory,
To the Adulteress, passion a vial
She might drink from before dying.

'Which role is the greatest,' and you look
To the King, his troubled succession;
To the Fool's ambivalent shadow,
To the mordant shadow of the Villain.

But I don't answer you.
I am struck dumb by the Extra
Who has turned away from the plot
And is gaping at the stage-flats,

As if he's just this minute realised.

Louise C. Callaghan

Skellig Michael

> *He who knows how cruel is sorrow*
> *for a companion understands: the paths of exile claim him.**

In the Boat

Rock companion for Little Skellig, three
quarters of an hour out from Portmagee.

Our boat like a shell on the sea,
motor-propelled, it rose and fell.

Boatman and me. The petticoat-swell
of a million sun-tipped waves.

Bird Sanctuary

> To
> our left
> like a ship,
> deck upon deck
> of shining, dark rock.
> Hanging mid-air like piano notes:
> gannet, storm-petrel, guillemot.
> Cliff-face graffiti. Ancient city of birds

Pilgrims

I start the climb,
an ascent the boatman said
of six hundred steps
Think heavenwards.

Seabirds in pairs
everywhere,
the only flower
a white-petal pannier.

Back and forth
the rock-laid path,
a stop for breath.
The sea below, slow

waves tipped in sunshine.
Climb and listen,
test the air.
Halfway there, footsteps,

names drop down to me:
Aristotle, Socrates, first causes
like bell-notes.
We nod on passing.

Monastic Settlement

The Seafarer, The Wanderer, early epithets
for solitude. I stair my way up
under a *lux aeterna* sky, stoop to enter:

Six cell houses – each one room for one,
a roofless chapel, and almost human, a standing stone.
As far West as one can go. Notched on the edge of dawn.

*From the Old English elegy 'The Wanderer', author unknown (translation by Louise C. Callaghan): 'Wat se pe cunnap / hu slipen bid sorg to geferan / pam pe him lyt hafad leofra geholena: / warad hine wraeclast.'

Celia de Fréine

Benchmark

Was it on that bench, beneath the weeping
birches, that one day an elderly man
asked if I liked animals? Black or bay
horses? Stallions, in particular, with
their great white seed-spurting pricks? I had seen
horses in films and knew they raced those times

father would disappear down a side-lane
and leave me staring into the window
of the shop that sold clothes for haybags
then reappear, a strange look on his face,
and in his fist, at times, the price of an ice
cream. The elderly man was quite horsey-

looking himself, with his tan skin and long
drippy nose. I watched as his eyes pursued
the boys from swing to slide to roundabout
then light on my brothers. I saw them roll
in the grass, become overwhelmed with
seeds of daisy, dandelion, and dock.

Celia de Fréine

Refugee

In the silence between news bulletins
I prayed for the children in Budapest
wondering what it would be like
to be dragged from a warm bed and bundled
onto the back of a cart. I thought of the toys
little girls had in books and watched as dolls
and teddy bears slipped from their owners' grasp.

The clang of metal reverberated
as the iron curtain forged its way round
that far country, like the melodeon doors
on Fox's Garage. In the shops there was
talk of the archbishop who'd had his toes
sliced off, of what he'd said but hadn't done.
Then one day my prayer was answered: a fresh-

faced girl with plaits and a pixie hood
arrived at our school. I brought her home
to show my mother, but my mother hid
in a wardrobe in the wireless room. I can still
remember that silence, where words that should
be spoken spiral upwards, forming globs
of condensation that map the rest of our lives.

Celia de Fréine

There was a soldier

I fell in love with him before I saw
him in uniform. He wasn't all that
handsome in uniform, but then he wasn't
all that handsome. When I went north to visit
him on leave he held me round the back
of the quarry and I thought I would melt
into putty that would spread and fill
the cracks in that ancient wall, that he
and I would inhabit there, become guardians
of that place where I had learned to swim
but all around me anemones clammed up.

Afterwards I thought about what it would
have been like to have had high tea
in the Imperial Hotel, leaned my arms
on the starched white tablecloth, felt the salt
against my skin as I lay back on the sheets.
I would have looked over his shoulder
to where his uniform wavered on the wardrobe
door and watched as the man he was struggled
against the shape of the man he would become,
just as the limbs of the condemned
convulse when the hangman tightens the noose.

Diane Fahey

Upstream

Light chevrons flat water; a shirtless
canoeist wears the morning on his back,
droplets firing the air as his paddle arcs.
I have tracked the river to where the mangroves
take hold and the bird life gets serious –
a kingfisher, totemic on a pole;
pelicans cruising low – three wing-beats then
a glide; sacred ibis gathered in a field
as if on a contemplative picnic.
In reedy nooks, lone fishermen dream up
hot dinners. I skirt their silence, guarding
my own which grows more spacious the further
I move from cars, lawn-mowers, dogs;
builds into an airy shell.

Estuary

Seahorse clouds, a fingernail's sliver
of moon. I wade through green swathes as if
reclaiming pieces of memory; as if
my brain were reconstituting itself –
cell by cell, rebuilding rooms; unlocking
others, long-sealed, to let this sea-light flow through.

My feet step from slurred prints, body tensing
before each wave with its rags of seaweed,
unseen flurries – sometimes a fleeting sting.
Out on the beach, the sky's a jigsaw this new tide
will fill in, spread to a silver-blue cloth.
Between low rocks, slash and eruption,
upsurge of chimerical white, chalices
of cloudless jade stilled to translucence.

Ann Egan

A Falcon's View

The first time I saw her
I was in that moment
Of pulling wingfeathers in,
To sheath my heart thump.

I was about to push
Claw against claw,
Stretch of scrawny skin,
Scrape of bone on bone.

My tailplumes veered to
The dreamshape of a flock
Of wild geese, nuisances
Of erring flightways.

My nail tips glistened,
Anticipation of sinking
In juice of fledgling flesh
Of one whin-gold gosling.

My eyes on its breastbeat,
Throb on throb with mine.
A passage of air all set
To part for my plunge.

Tongue curdling for blood,
When east of my duckling
I spotted a cloud,
White as new milk,

Fallen clear of the sky,
Strolling, not floating, covering
The green gold Curragh.
I saw her in her standing.

All white as that apparition,
Moss glints in her grey eyes,
Toss of hazel brown hair,
Twitch of belly laughs on her lips.

Beyond all, it was her stillness.
She was, you could say just like
Me as I prepare my swoop
From the cloak of the heavens.

She stood on her sod, gazing.
Clench gone from my claws,
I stayed poised in her watch.
Couldn't say if the chick,

Wispy feathers and berried flesh,
Hobbled to earth or sky.
For I held my hold.
I found Brigid of the Curragh.

Paul Grattan

Maxim
in memory of Hywel Thomas, philosopher

And if we should be refused trousers
or find ourselves foutering under stars,
exiled by grocers' daughters, in Cuban
heels, a high-heel without curves, better
to have been tarred and feathered in the great
balloon fire of 1785 than suffer this closure,
half out of our patent leathered minds.

You kill me, roaring, tautologies of fuchsia
and blackthorn have emptied our bellies,
binding our hyperborean arse cracks to the wind.
My manqué, my melancholic manqué, go on
in your virtue, save the wails, the wind eggs
and a thousand dule-tree flowers, for the want
of a kind word, John Knox looking on.

Paul Grattan

Descartes at Ibrox
for Martin Mooney

Check him, some waster waxing lyrical in a bar,
chinned by a bear in Rangers colours for failing
to hum ardently the air to *Derry's Walls*; this *per se*
would not seem unusual. Except it didn't happen

Qua rammy. Injuries were sustained as a result
of paper cuts to the left nostril, inflicted when said Hun
proclaimed Hume's rebuttal of the French Man to be
epistemologically speaking, *fucking out of order*.

Coming to, reverse angle replays show two tattooed
fists insist on their existence, above and beyond the temple
of the Copeland Road Stand. Man marked, out the game
the upward trajectory of his meditations proved fatal.

T.F. Griffin

After Late Summer Separation

A long autumn. Snowing leaves out
As she moved from his orbit.

Tired-tongued between world imagined summer,
World real with mid-air leaves

Touching the hair
Of walking lovers,

The eye catches the sun's burn
And stares.

Sheep chewing there
With no abstraction –

A song now
Without double standard:

(A church clock ringing three
As reality sustains itself)

And this is introspection in a changed season,
Not depression of winter.

And in one room, curled foetus shaped
In the heartland of desire,

Silence, and the pounding imposition of otherness.

T.F. Griffin

I Wanted to Hear your Voice

I wanted to hear your voice
Above the silence
Of the posed face;
Of the man in blue
With the wry smile
And the nudge of knowing
Curtained in doubt.

I wanted to hear your voice
Uncertain;
I needed an open smile,
A face to tell a dry courtesan
Of dead spirits
About circles
Around enigmas;

I wanted to hear your voice
Above the loudest abstraction;

I wanted to hear your voice
Clean and clear.

Heather Jones

The Last Chapter of the Toraíocht: Gráinne mourns Diarmuid

A conglomerate of misshapen sequence,
Black Auvergnat in strength,
Tusks as nails, irredeemable, inchoate –
Marking where the boar killed him.
Pictures in a darkening room
Hung to harken light –
The news, an axis of whispers,
Dimly painted.

In these walls, her skirts alive as froth,
She may remember moving softly,
Fearing to break, ornaments,
Balconied in *Memento mori*
Splendour,
Not her own.

Now she recalls, in trampled prayer,
A bruise he had one time
Or that sodden tempera blacked eye
Of willow flesh.
Yet supplemental detail,
Healing then, salt raw,
For he lived still.

Michael Murphy

Passage West

*My father said that people who were drowned in the river
were carried home on a door.*

Coming off the street
a gust tries to butt us.

When we turn our heads,
wrong-foot the wind,
a clap of suds rises on the steps.

The river overlaps the wall,
where just beyond,
the current turns in its sleep.

My mother takes us
by the spare of our coats,
drags us back from the edge.

At the far side of the quay,
two boys with monkey arms are leaning
for driftwood.

We are shifting against the gale,
salt spraying,
all sound blocked in our ears.

Out-stretched, the boy has gone over,
broken through glass
to the other side.

She holds a plank,
brings him back, ropes his arm
from its socket.

Tonight, laid flat,
I follow the procession, sense the heat
of a lamp creeping up my sleeve.

Margaret O'Shea

I Stand To The North Of Her Always In Shadow

A skirting autumn wind
Spun me drunk with lust
Into the throw-over of bracken,
To ferment in loamy soil,
In the small hours
Of the impending Millennium.
I am the green stick
In the close-knit wood.

I stand to the North of her
Always in shadow.

In May she's a top-heavy girl.
For June she wears a new face.
In September, a Persian rug.
Even the December frown
Of brown suits her.

I stand to the North of her
Always in shadow.

The wind plays peek-a-boo in her.
Rain specks bejewel her.
Sunshine winks at her.
Snow makes a crystal chandelier
Of her.

I stand to the North of her
Always in shadow.

Her skin has a glisten of resin,
With the grain and grit
Of untanned hide,
She sings to herself at Equinox
And twiddles her thumbs all winter.

I stand to the North of her
Always in shadow.

Red Deer in rut itch their flanks
And bucks buff their velvets on her side,
She houses a crow's nest on her oxter
And tingles at the land and
Take-off of birds feet.
A snagged rope swings from her.

I stand to the North of her
Always in shadow.

No bow-saw buck-saw chain-saw
Or burrowing weevil
Ever nicked or notched her.
No clap of lightening split her
Nor black frost cracked her.

I stand to the North of her
Always in shadow.

The mistletoe and ivy
She wears as laurels,
Grope their sickly way
Within an arm's reach of me.
I hear them hunger to choke me.

I stand to the North of her
Always in shadow.

Briars crackle
At my scrunched toes,
My breath is short.
My sap is a sop
As she creeps to haunt
The moon,
My grip is shallow
As a fingerprint,
I'm losing ground
At every rustle
And stir;

If you don't die back. Mother.
If you don't die back.

Maureen Oliphant

She is under the weeping willow

She is under the weeping willow, my daughter,
not playing hide and seek, not making daisy chains.

She is under the weeping willow, my daughter,
not engaged in girlish chatter, not braiding her friend's hair.

She is under the weeping willow, my daughter,
not whispering sweet nothings, not promising to obey.

She is under the weeping willow, my daughter,
By the lych-gate in the shadow of a Victorian church.

A busy highway passes, there's a lively Inn next door,
on the hillside a children's playground, laughter.

Two days living, then buried in a communal grave,
my baby daughter, under the weeping willow.

A collection of many sorrows, a stranger stops
and strews wild flowers, a daisy for my daughter.

William Scammell

Heft

The heft, the haft, the shaft
of the axe, the ankle, calf
muscle and polished thigh
of the axe, its cut and thrust,
its invitation to the waltz,
the grin of the edge, the recidivist
lump at the back of the head,
the creak of oak, spit of sap,
split skirt of bark,
the high cheekbones, Luluesque
pallor, hard knock hips,
the sheer stocking tops,
the hammer horror of the axe
caught in a fix, a cleft stick –
the bondage of labour, and
the sweetly humped back.

Litany

Peace to their flat tweed caps,
their battered pickups, their 1930s
trousers and turn-ups, their waiting dogs,
humble as a patchwork rug.
Peace to the golem of their noses
pitted against all the devils above and below,
the ambivalent nods, the odds and sods
of jobs that are born needing doing again.
Peace to the ammoniac stench of piss
that moats the barn in winter,
the infinite spaces of the rain-barrel,
cobblestones hunched down for the long haul.
Peace to the long hours in his head,
the naked light bulb in the yard.

Che Qianzi

Souvenirs
translation from the Chinese by Ouyang Yu

life holds meetings, death gives souvenirs

hair cut, heads
are souvenirs picked up
in the rubbish dump abandoned
pencils are picked up

life holds meetings, death gives souvenirs

neatly dressed
bodies are well kept souvenirs
"want to have a look? get undressed first!"
exchanging souvenirs, exchanging angles

life holds meetings, death gives souvenirs

fake and unlucky souvenirs
chastity: souvenir hard to keep

life holds meetings, death gives souvenirs

two people have been quarrelling all day
in order to
leave poisonous souvenirs

life holds meetings, death gives souvenirs

put a nail through the palm
in order to
find the souvenir of the scar

life holds meetings, death gives souvenirs

writing poetry; burning
a poem when written
is like the ashes of the dead, not much when collected

life holds meetings, death gives souvenirs
"no-one wants 'em, play for yourself!"

Ah Jian

Missing the Past is also a Life
translation from the Chinese by Ouyang Yu

making one's own cotton-padded jackets and making one's own
                                    dough for *mantou*
missing grand-ma's hands beating me up and caressing me
the then trams are more lovely than the now air-planes
those old photos that smell of pickled vegetables
like small windows, the ancient times outside the windows
the ancient times only 30 years ago
as if you could get it if you pushed open the windows; the
                                    furthest is the closest

moved by the details of those days
you close ajar your eyes and everything is back
use again that *ah yi*'s shanghai scented soap
lick clean that three-cent ice-sucker
talking to girls in the *shitang* where adults held a dancing party
the stars then were eyes of angels

missing the past, the real life
like ruminating, the first round is the taste of the past
and the second is genuine nutrition

time stays there for always, extending into the past and
                                    the future
you can go into the future with body and soul but only soul into
                                    the past
we often return there, to have fun
but can't stay there without coming out

mantou: steamed bread.
ah yi: the common way children address adult women in mainland China.
shitang: canteen or mess hall attached to a work unit, still common in China.

Geoffrey Squires

from 'Untitled Poem'

That move sometimes and are sometimes still
what they are each one only what it is
this or because

Itself itself always itself
ahead of itself   in advance of itself
already   before

and superimposed as it were

Movement in some part   somewhere   of the foliage
close by or near

profusion of vegetation
rich dense   thickly arrayed

soft green of leaf of bower of place

Seeing what we see what is seen

and it is all there instantly at a moment's notice
completeness of world nothing lacking or missing
no part to be filled in
each detail small particular

Looking back up where we came down from
difficult now to see how

a steep slope dotted with scrub
small plants clinging
to the broken face
dry and wiry
stone crumbling
fissures and cracks and ledges and here and there
small parcels of soil of ground

and the little stream at the bottom
glinting in the sunlight
whose noise rose up to us   quite loud
reaching us in that other world
of great space and emptiness
of birds wheeling in nothingness

Continuity   of a kind

although it is difficult to say exactly of what
world   things in their place

How difficult it would be to draw this
when it already looks as if it has been drawn
sketched out by someone else

broken lines marks traces   discontinuities
as if things have been altered or erased

and which seems haphazard almost careless
at the level of detail until one stands back
and takes in the whole

impressions of hollows   small obscurities
the occasional smudge of bushes here and there
or a blank space where the rock face is quite smooth

no boundaries real edges   a general lack of definition
nothing quite finished or complete
leaving it to the observer the viewer
to round things off supply what is missing

Reminder of something something that happened
what led to it what flowed from it
what happened as a result of it

Passivity of long journeys
where the landscape changes and changes again
once one gets clear of the city

a river veering away
followed by its canal
low hills in the distance

and the nearer detail
washing hanging out on a line
behind some farm cottages
cars waiting at level crossings
children waving   small huts
a man digging his garden
who does not even look up

And to get it to concentrate on any one thing
for any length of time
requires a considerable effort a discipline a reining in
which does not seem quite right

Behind that and behind that again
world always layered   tiered

a small wood a copse
at the bend in the river
between green fields   distance
judgement   a road zig-zagging towards the horizon

Or like something that one might carry
take up and bear away
except that it seems so light sometimes so immaterial

Behind that and behind that again

and comes back quickly re-establishes itself
after the momentary lapse

which is in itself difficult to explain
a kind of absence perhaps

but wholly   completely   everything settled instantly
in its place   exactly where it was before

and nothing it seems has changed
in that moment when it was not subject to this unremitting
                                                attention
no movement that occurred or if it did
was so small so quickly rectified
that one has no way of knowing
if it happened at all

Nothing but what

mountains in the distance hills
a road here and there
stubble fields smoke blowing across
sky blue turning to empty

By which   of which

A slight delay a momentary pause an idea

rustle of vegetation
not watching but   not listening but

memory ground to which we return
some peculiar configuration of the senses

Robert Welch

Crosshaven: Neptune Calms the Sea
adapted from Virgil's Aeneid, Book 1

It's off the Point, and the sky is turbid and remorseless;
but even worse, with each vertiginous slide and hurtle
of waves that aren't waves but dark mountainous shiftings,
the warrior and his stricken sailors can see the actual sea-floor.
Neptune, at last, breaks surface, and thrusts his serene face
through the racing turbulence; he roars at Aeolus and tells him
to get the fuck back to Sicily and to keep his winds where
they belong, in the stones and caves that darken all that coast,
and to hold them there until the time comes when he is told
to let them out, by him, and not by anyone with points to score.
Even before he's finished shouting the sea quietens, the heaving
waves calm down, and the god, dispersing the thickened fog,
allows the sun to filter back, but slowly. And now Triton, his son,
along with the sea-nymph, Cymothoe, push the ships off
jagged reefs, each one groaning as it thunders back down,
Neptune steering them with his trident, opening up
the newly-risen sandbanks, meanwhile always making sure
the water keeps as still as he has willed it to become.
Then, at last, the light wheels spinning cleanly, he guides
his chariot away across the surface of the sea towards America.

Fred Johnston

The Black Birds
i.m. Caitlín Maude

What are we doing
Behind the rock,
The sun going out in the sea,
Night coming down like sleep?

The weather drowned
In the mad water –
Our cracked hands' skin,
Bombers in the Kerry air

The drone of black birds
At four in the morning,
Crawling over our thin roof,
Laying death on the far poor –

Potassium iodate pills,
Our National Emergency Plan:
Keep out of Reach of Children –
We see, hear, say, nothing.

A nuclear croon, a hot
Vision-poem dreamed by
A madman: our nibs melt
In the heat of our shame.

Is this what we are,
Crouched like children
Behind a sinking rock,
In a bog of words and more words?

Fred Johnston

Folk Song

What I sing when I crave other people,
The joining in of them, crude and shapeless
But true to them, singing for the sake of it.

Shapeless a song with no one singing it,
Out of shape a room with no tune in it –
Sad the sound of your own voice, sometimes.

George Seferis

Erotikos Logos
translation from the Greek by Maria Ypsilanti

For there is among mankind a kind of person most foolish,
who despises what is at hand and strains the eyes on what is far away,
chasing the impossible with vain hopes.
– Pindar

I

Rose of Fate, you sought to wound us; like a wave
you bent, like the redemption of a secret word;
and beautiful was the command you chose and gave
beautiful was your smile all like the ready sword.

The ascent of your cycle revived again all nature
and our thoughts were driven from your thorn astray,
our impulse dawned naked to find and capture
your grace; the world was easy: a rhythm simple and gay.

II

The secrets of the sea lie on the shore forgotten,
the sea-bed's darkness lies forgotten on the foam;
the corals, purple flashes suddenly, begotten
by memory... stir it not... hark to its sounds that roam

lightly... you touched the apple-tree – blooms softly quiver –
hand reaches out, the leading thread goes on and on...
Dark shiver in the root and in the leaves... dark shiver,
could it be you that brought back the forgotten dawn!

Full open ripe days the bosom of the skies;
now in the field of parting lilies bloom anew...
A trembling light reflected only in those eyes,
soul appearing pure in the air like song, like dew.

Was it night that shut its eyes? A soot, a sound
remains like a bowstring's the distant din;
ashes and vertigo on the sea-shore, black all round,
and a dense fluttering that hides surmise within.

Rose of the wind, you took us; we asked not why
as mind was building bridges of a mystic height,
as fingers met and as two destinies passed by
and poured themselves out in the low and rested light.

III

Dark shiver in the root and in the leaves! Delay
no more...Show sleepless form in the rich silence when
you raise your head from the curve of your hands; and may
your will be done so that I hear you tell me again

the words that touched and joined the blood like an embrace;
and let your longing spread like shadow in the mart
and let your lavish tresses flood us from the lace
of every kiss to the recesses of the heart.

Your eyes lowered; on your lips you had the smile
humbly recounted by painters of old.
Forgotten page, reading from an ancient bible,
I heard your voice breathe and such light speech unfold:

"The fleeting time is silent and soft and unworldly
as pain rows and rows in my soul tenderly,
dawn breaking the sky, and it is as if some fragrant
bushes are passing by; the dream sinks not in the sea.

A sudden startle in the eyes, blushing over the body,
a flock of doves wakes and descends; entangled I am in such
a low movement of the wings that go around, around:
the crowd of stars in my bosom is a human touch.

A shell against my ear now roars the lament
of the world, adverse and distant and confused and lonely;
but these are moments and they fade, and what remains to reign
is the reflection of my yearning, my yearning only.

As if I'd risen naked in a taken remembrance
when you came, familiar stranger, beloved, to bend
at my side and give me the immeasurable deliverance
that I once hoped the wind's quick sistrum would send..."

The shattered sunset slowly faded away;
futile it seemed to ask the gifts of heaven. Still
your eyes lowered. Thorn of the moon, a ray
bloomed and you started at the shadows of the hill.

Our love inside the mirror grows smaller now
school of forgetfulness the visions in the cup
of sleep, and in the depths of time how narrow, how
lost is our heart in the cradle of some other lap...

IV

Two lovely serpents, tentacles of separation
crawl in the night of the trees and seek to meet
a love now lost in the chambers of desolation;
sleepless they ever search, they neither drink nor eat.

Twisting, bending, spinning, their insatiable mind
grows bigger, spreads its rings, makes of our body its nest;
the body that the laws of the starry dome bind
and animate its fervent force never at rest.

Against the shivering wood now leans the night
and silence is a silver cup where moments fall;
a careful chisel carves bold lines: there stands upright
a figure as the counter strokes sound clear and whole.

The statue flashes suddenly. The bodies fade
away in the wind the rain the sun the sea.
Who knows how the beauties of our world are made,
who knows if a soul slept in eternity.

The parted serpents go round in imagination
(the forest shines with flower, bird, with sprout and leaf)
their wavy searching still remains, like the rotation
of the eternal wheel that gives birth to our grief.

V

Where is the day that changed it all, the double-edged day?
Shall we ever find a river to go downstream?
Shall we ever find a sky to drop its dew of May
in our soul reared by the lotus in a dream?

Upon the rock of patience we wait and wait
for a miracle to unlock heavens and make once more
everything possible, as an angel guards the gate
of the ancient palace, and the blossoms evening bore

vanish...Red rose of the wind and fate, alone
you are left in memory, a grave rhythm, a ripple
in the garment of night, swell of the sea, now gone,
swell of a purple, storm and breeze...The world is simple.

Trevor Joyce

Love Songs from a Dead Tongue
for George Hitching

Note: These poems are worked from originals, some dating back at least to the fifteenth century and perhaps several centuries earlier. They speak in the voice of the famous queen, Gormlaith (died 948 AD), whose three husbands were all kings, the last being Niall Blackknee who, in 919, died in battle with the Norse.

Six of the poems were committed to writing only in 1839, by a country schoolteacher. Understandably, there are many corruptions following such long and difficult transmission, and scholars have noted the variability of tone and register.

I have made no attempt to echo the rhyme-scheme of the originals, preserving from their Bardic apparatus only the quatrain-structure and the repetition of the (approximate) start-word at the end of each poem. My primary interest has been to carry over their power and sense of personal force, and the interplay of self-possession with possessions and hierarchy.

The texts and versions are those provided by Osborn Bergin and Anne O'Sullivan. My thanks to Máire Herbert for advice and support. Bracketed ellipses in the text refer to lines which are lost or obscure.

1

Grief in the king-fort?
With Niall gone, small wonder;
all was fast against affliction,
grievous now.

And will grieve on
abandoned by civility,
though a dynasty outlasted
loneliness from there.

All kings but one
in time relinquish rule.
Who'd want the world?
Grief in the king-fort,
               grief.

2

Laughter across the way marks out
the marriage-house;
such loud excess
intrudes a desolation here.

Though happily that bride
may get what she contracted for
some are short-changed
as I hereby lay charge.

You, ruler of the lasting world,
I now denounce,
for killing of my kind, my gentle
loving and most innocent king.

As hostage he'd be worth
thoroughbred herds, goldhoards;
who brought him here would learn
my further kindnesses.

Proper to ransom such a man
could to me show him so kind
delivering me from a one-day's raid
some twelve score head of beef.

Delicate linens, ah! you break
my heart, you, where Niall could sleep sound,
and you, white one, little bed,
you miss him too.

How then should I bear myself
happening upon a shirt
when he it dressed
lies dead in Kells?

Travelling westward from Armagh
Niall put me this:
whichever goes in front,
my love, where should we head?

Straight answer, this, my king,
together in the cool clay
of Ailech, let them lay us
in a single grave.

If you, my love, go first,
in front of me into the earth,
I'll take myself no other queen
but long grieving without laughter
                    without laughter.

3

Kells, occasion for blindness,
since I lay with your King;
Kells, grown disfigured
now Niall is gone.

The first kings I wived,
I augmented their glory,
but Niall was far dearer than both;
Kells, occasion for blindness.

My bright Niall ceased,
my man and my king ceased,
here his broad lands continue;
Kells, occasion for blindness.

Well I remember generous Niall
here on this hill
laughing his wealth away;
Kells, occasion for blindness.

I will walk to the grave of Niall;
there is room where he lies
for me to lie next him;
Kells, occasion for blindness,
                              blindness.

4

Breaks the heart keening
as the edge keen the king,
keen Niall Blackknee
gracious as great.

[...]

Ask what breaks my heart:
keening Niall the bright laughing;
till doomsday the heart hurt
atrociously wasting.

First I came into Munster:
high-king's consort queen
to arch-bishop Cormac
the perfectly-bright.

Then next into Leinster
in which rich realm
though some muttered
I did not starve.

[...]

... came Tara's heir,
that true prince,
successor to arch-kings.

Together we shared
childhood in Tara,
concentric city
of the true promised land.

That destroyer of pastures,
that master of plunder,
that fiercest of men,
deepest red amongst Irish.

The place where he fell
broke my heart
[...]
nor does Donal survive him.

Niall, king, son of kings,
Donal, soft face unfurrowed,
dead detach me from kin,
reduce heart to sheer blood.

I am Gormlaith, the keening:
first husband-king Cormac,
son Donal, fierce Niall,
these three broke my heart.

O King of the stars,
grant mercy to Niall,
O Mary, great queen,
shield this cold keening
                        breaks.

5

An empty fort
is forewarning to others;
such desolation in a palace
just one trick among life's many.

I miss the princes
hospitable and brave
and grieve
through so much emptiness.

Soon the rest
will make joint desolation;
is this not sign enough?
an empty fort;
········empty.

6

Rag, patched on patch,
why would I blame you?
not one courtly hand
added craft to your stitch.

In Tara once
alongside Niall of Emain,
happily he honoured me:
I drank from his own cup.

In Limerick once
with loving Niall of Ailech,
my clothes spectacular
among the western chieftains.

When his people gathered
to test their foals for speed
I drank as they drank, wine
from fine horn cups.

Seven score women attended us
in these assemblies
as the race was settled
on the green course of my king.

I am a woman of Leinster,
I am a woman of Meath;
ask which land most dear to me:
no zone of those, but my true king's north.

Brambles snare me,
snarl my rags;
thorn no ally,
briar attacks,
        rag.

7

Mourning Niall I survive;
what pain could exceed this?
surplus such days,
me so disfigured.

Bone-weary tonight, I,
all love-words exhausted;
draped Tara quenched too,
all glamour gone out.

Emain silent and dark
where they played once,
hosts gathered
departed.

Utter silence in Oileach:
no music;
Lough Foyle's speech is hoarse;
disfigured, I die.

To the west to the east
each kingdom enfeebled,
it grieves me
their grief.

Sad this north too
my voice strange to its soldiery;
the south dwindles away,
grief blurs my face.

My king, son of kings,
who gave away gold,
dead, stuns the woods;
grief endures.

King Niall Blackknee, his queen,
master of armies, his consort,
now has gossip for counsel;
do you question my
mourning?

8

Ah! grief my own,
Ah! lost my own love,
destroyed in the night
that king's son went down.

Ah! queen's son set below,
Ah! then what future after,
as giving as brave falls
and the field falls waste after?

Ah! true king now dead
that alive was not halt;
this soul fallen in war,
I chant pity and pain
                      Ah!

9

Here the hound is neglected
till proven,
the unloved
easily slighted.

The crow's black, say I say,
then, white, they say back;
I go wrong, the same say,
whether striding or bowed.

Bleak the hill without trees,
chill the shoulder unfriended,
and empty the weave without issue,
here, don't I know it?

As she finds in love
from one man satisfaction,
no he ever found
but one woman could please.

That king son of kings, was my pleasure,
most loved and most brave, that most gentle man
stood head against head
with this child of the arch-king.

I a long age since
in this fort of crude strength,
my force fragile, this frail I,
can't abide
        here.

10

Soft with that foot, Monk,
you stand by a king's side
shovelling covers
on limbs I lay next to.

An age in that dark, Monk,
you've gravelled him down;
an age in his night
he shrinks from the boards.

That son of free giving
earned better than crosses;
sheet him over with stone
but soft with that foot, Monk.

The queen that chants this,
gentle daughter of kings,
craves that stone for her bed-sheet
so soft with that foot, Monk,
                       soft.

11

Pity the earth constrains you, Niall,
pity us visit your grave!
status and grace stand annulled
now north holds the north's king dead.

A while with the meek,
a while with the mighty;
better than these whiles my while with Niall
who laughed as he drank.

I had banquets with wine,
I had wealth and society;
now Niall walks with saints
what could prevent him Heaven?

Bright but for black knee
Niall had no equal;
such beauty!
the curl, the grey eye.

Now the surge breaks cold,
the wind storms from the west,
generosity sinks to her knees,
the ship shudders.

Fair switches with foul,
harsh wind knows no ceasing,
bud is blasted on branch
just by this death.

Where was joy sits decay;
hard threnody this:
my friend in his blood,
Tara ruined till the world's end,
                              the pity!

12

Sighing heavy tonight, God!
heaviest yet;
for loss of the son of my own bright Niall
alive I'd walk under the earth.

All friends dwindle and fade
now that Niall is dimmed
the listening ear
hears no laughter.

Note these dead:
father mother and brothers,
and foster-kin, loved and revered,
dead and buried and gone.

Fair one held me high
over vatfulls of gold,
fed me nothing but honey,
count that fair one dead too.

Account also the young
who smiled on my knee
while I gave them a love
as if blood of my blood.

So many have gone
from the yellow-topped earth
yet this grieves me most:
Donal's cheek stroked with clay.

Though weakness and war
hunt the living
this value survives:
the love of the child of your blood.

Sorrow on her
trusts her son
to the care
of the foolish.

Grief on her
sent her son
into chaos
of waters and men.

Donal, son of bright Niall,
and of twelve generations of kings,
those lovers of verse
now past moving.

The child of such ancestry
darkens the sky;
white his hand, white his foot,
my heart heavy
           sighing.

13

Preach, priest!
with quick benediction
on the great soul
of him, the well-born.

Scholars and clerks
had regard in his reign;
hearsay truly reported
his charity.

Not my boast but Niall's will:
that three hundred horse,
with ten hundred cows
I gave in one day.

Generality dealt with,
his sage sought my gift:
cattle, three hundred head,
cloth, a rich crimson bolt.

I paid off his poets
enough and excess;
may what they then received
serve now his soul.

Sorrow afflict him who sundered us
while yet I lived,
sorrow on him seized my horseman
left me alone.

Sorrow on him struck asunder
my dear friend and myself
would have been in his debt
had he left us as one.

Mark, priest, this my poem,
since a while we are private;
let ear hold what it catch,
then rise, priest, and
                         preach!

14

Say, three times thirty,
nine times nine, I've loved,
yet if I now loved twenty more
still it wouldn't satisfy.

For Niall I left
all other loves,
desiring his desire;
who might detain me then?

Among assembled warriors
all trophies fell to him;
yet, encountering such straits,
better I'd loved some serf.

Elaborate cloaks, golden rings,
and strings of thoroughbreds;
broad flood run down to drought,
his goods all gone.

Between heaven and earth,
a white dress and a black cloak
now my sole provisioning;
in Kells of the hundred kings, I starve.

North of the church on Sabbath day
instructed by the gentle touch
of the left hand of my king
I, to the abbot's wife, gave goods.

An orb with golden ornament,
fat cows, two score,
a blue Norse hood, a case of horn,
and thirty ounce of gold.

And she, who has them yet,
repaid me them tonight:
two measures of hard oats,
two eggs from her vast clutch.

By him who lit the sun's fire,
if my Niall of the Black Knee lived,
then, you, you minor abbot's twist,
I'd need no eggs from you!

A roan horse,
a cup, and other articles of gold,
I gave her once, and was returned
a cap, a comb, some sundry pretty cloth.

Wretched be the falsely proud,
wretched they who hoard;
before misfortune struck
remember, poets took my gold.

Who would trade horses
for good verse, may God reward;
if I speak well of Niall, think
what could a poet say, for pay!
                    what say?

15

Wretched to me
my own homeland,
I'd sooner stay in Ulster
conversing with kings.

Through seventeen years
among this aristocracy
they have dealt with me kindly,
rather kinsfolk than strangers.

I and the mountain lark,
of a muchness our nature:
with the wood within reach
she sleeps in the peat-bog.

Getting so much from Niall
what reason to leave him?
that gentle slender-handed man,
unequalled.
[...]
               ...wretched.

16

Niall! pray heaven on his soul!
let every priest pray too;
he knew life's worth,
and my heart, lacking him, grows sick.

That wise head the land obeyed
can't cancel now my grief:
such the incalculable loss;
his speech to me was soft.

His speech to me was sweet:
such the incalculable loss;
I have no taste for words
but beating fists unceasingly.

Beating fists unceasingly,
his death my extreme loss;
and though in triumph he went out,
bitter our affliction now.

Bitter our affliction now
the very churches weep for him;
myself can't limit grief
though enemies deride.

Though enemies deride,
though solidarity lend strength,
with Niall laid low
how now live on?

How now live on
lacking passion, joy and song?
He who withheld no wealth for self
to mourn demeans each woman well.

Niall! pray heaven on his soul!
to survive him is protracted pain,
that stranger to our company
till judgement day:
               Niall!

17

Lamentation has its season
and right end, even for gentle Niall;
excess has delivered me
to this not life not death.

A time of one and thirty years,
since that king died,
each night I wept him
seven hundred tears.

Last night he, my dead king, came in,
said: put an end to mourning, love,
the Arch-King of the seraphim
grows weary hearing you.

I turned on Niall,
angry as I had never been before,
said: for what cause should that highest King
turn weary from a penitent?

Remember, love, he said,
God set all men in being;
why then would he wish
to overhear them weeping?

Then Niall himself
turned from me, twisting love;
at sight of this I scream aloud,
spring after him.

For some support
I leaned my breast
against a bed-post of smooth yew
which penetrated it, my heart.

Tonight I implore God
grant me surcease in death;
on what road Niall turns
let me turn too.

King husband first
three hundred cows,
two hundred horse
conveyed me.

Then my second husband king,
never to seem outdone
in generosity of soul,
conveyed me double that.

Why should I hide
from my true king, these gifts?
Such gifts, and twice such more,
Niall gave me in one month.
                    Lamentation.

Tom Mac Intyre

Visiting Hours

Plump with the word,
The Whoopers of April
are flown away north;

finding them gone,
we ship oars,
let her drift...

Chinese? Russian? Possibly. Some
dandruff scribe of The Gael? Name
it, on closer scrutiny, talisman
insufficient to stay the visit –
second visit – of the black swan,
the first long-ago birthday gift:
groomed silhouette, course set,
she rode, buoyant, a compliant Acheron,
the serial silence, four-poster post-
post-modern, for you, you alone.

Second time 'round, a more direct
approach, we've met, after all. Out,
out of the hill-folk sky she comes,
document – cavalierly, almost –
in gob, split-second hover, flings
it at you, *caveat* as javelin,
jug-jug it sings, jugular bound.

Theodicies of time, mercy, dolour.
She swops plumage, welcome white.
Seven cygnets, sinecure and cynosure,
ply the bog-lake of the heart,
seven for starters, by the sixth week
five, later three, finally a pair.
A list of the accused might run:
pike, mink, several kinds of hawk,
the fox, even. No one can tell.

Piecemeal, this opens to perturbation
as summer fattens the reed-bunting,
cat's-tail soars, parents thrive,
she – the carer born, he
supportive fore and aft, both –
to an inconsequential tune –
serene. By September I knew.
'They're all here', she said, 'You
can't see them – but they're here'.

Now I find her in a shore-cave.
Comfortable in white and grown
prodigiously, she broods. The heap –
raft – of driftwood is throne.
Come close, the dark eyes invite.
I advance. Steps make no sound,
silence in this place a censer
glow. She nods me closer, closer
still. I lay a lonesome head
on the pillow of swan's-down,
her neck descends, unconscionably
mild, enfolds me, and I sleep.

Tom Mac Intyre

The Healer's Daughter

Lover's London post-card - 'Detail
from Klimt's *Medicine*, destroyed
nineteen fortyfive'. There you are,
spacey shimmer of amber and red,
bowl in raised left hand, your
temple-snake eats from the bowl,
we're back where we started.

That *L*-shaped room, *metteur
en scéne* in you hitting it
on the button, right-turn ex-
tension, a here, a there, no stick
of furniture, walls rinsed white.
We commenced – remember – where
such rooms decree, quotidian
lower bar of the *L*, come in,
lovely day, fond of the rain,

isn't it? *Cinnte*. I start to babble
An Bunnán Buí, when in trouble
fall back on the poor bittern,
'*sé mo léan do luí*' - 'Know it?'
Comeuppance condign. 'Sure.
Much translated, ever been translated
yourself?' And you lead me,

you of the gentle hands, ante-
room to arena, ninety degree
turn; deep in the airy perpend-
icular of the *L*, we meet for
good and earnest. I weigh in
at an ounce, all bridges down,
as the snake you wore, necklace,
unclasps, slips to the floor,

merry there begins to play –
child, kitten, pup, otter –
in jig time floor to air,
fix on me, approach, flicks –
on a U-turn – my cheek, back
to you, nests about your throat.
That's it. My breath's scant.

I'd have given myself *C minus*,
possibly *D* - yet your invitation
stood, unfathomable patience,
sustenuto green of the postman's van
in which I'm borne to the river,
eyes directed to the water,
surface-stir- shape - an eel?
no eel - *Ecce*! - substantial
you in the elements of your glory,

polished scales brown, biege, fawn,
lozenge pattern, circles within,
you strut your stuff, 'Pale one,
la morsure originale, c'est moi'
ripple, furl, stretch, siren
sigh. 'Your call. *Ce soir*, say?'
Ever been courted like this, man?
Odalisque liquid on liquid divan.

Wall-eyed child of the kirk,
Hygeia, I again sue for pardon.
When you found the way to my bed –
when my hand met your exotic cold –
there are many things I've done
I would a thousand times unmake.
Meanwhile, I doss anywhere, sleepwalk
with the herd, wonder, wonder,
Mighty Daughter, when may I awake?

Michael S. Begnal

It Gets Dark, the Elements

Finally, in blue black events, the event,
bars of Galway night,
it gets dark, the elements
unfurling our beautiful minds

beautiful freedom in them,
the three of us
crossing oceans crossing lakes
the dark horizon,
tremendous bodies of water
are always there
and we swim that power

knowing each other's minds

I am glad our bodies hold freedom like
events events stretched our muscles,
we screwed the law, three far from home,
and that our swaying bodies united us,
that we lay inarticulate on a shore

the medium is the message

Yael Globerman

She Returns
translated from the Hebrew by Karen Alkalay-Gut

She goes home again to close
the door behind her body.
Night that broke in
bursts from the room
aiming a shiny silence at her.
She knows the black hose
it wears on its face. Those
she picked up from the carpet
in the hotel room. They're hers.
She stands in the doorway. The floor
sprawls before her.

Karen Alkalay-Gut

Metamorphosis

Franz and I are having coffee at Nona café.
It wasn't something we planned –
I spotted him with those bat ears
leaning over an espresso
clearly in the throes
of a panic attack
and moved to his table.

He barely notices me,
watches the braless girls
in their short t-shirts
going one way,
and a suspicious boy in a coat
walking back.

In Prague he said
I knew my enemy.
It was them
and it was me.
Here it's so much more
interrelated.

Caitlín Maude

An Mháthair

'Ní fíor go bhfeiceann tú os do chomhair
seanbehan liath seargaithe,
gan luas géag
ná mire meangan,
tite i bhfeoil.
Bhí mé óg, ach tá mé níos óige –
álainn, tá mé anois níos áille fós.
Nach bhfeiceann tú an triúr?
Gile na finne, na duibhe, na doinne –
mo thriúr mac, mo thriúr Oscar.
Féach an mhaorgacht i mo shúil,
an uaisleacht i mo ghnúis,
an óige,
an áille,
an luas,
an neart,
chuile bhua faoi thrí.
Is triúr fear óg mé,
luathláidir cumasach,
agus fós,
is triúr maighdean mé
i ngrá le triúr ógfhear –
maighdeanacha meidhreacha meangacha,
snadhmaithe i scáilí deoracha úra
aisteacha na coille –
an eala, an fiach dubh, an smólach
ag coraíocht i mo cheann.
Nach bhfeiceann tú na hógfhir
agus na maighdeanacha
agus iad ag caint, ag gáirí
agus ag gabháil fhoinn,
in ngreim láimhe ina chéile
ag dul síos an boithrín
fada fada síoraí
agus an t-ór ag spréacharnaíl
ar gach taobh díobh?'

Nuala Ní Chonchúir

The Mother *(translation of Caitlín Maude's 'An Mháthair')*

'This is no shrivelled, silver-haired crone
you see before you,
slow-gaited
and mad-mouthed,
gone to pot.
I was young once, now I'm younger –
stunning, now more stunning still.
Can't you see this trio?
The blonde, the raven-haired, the dun-locked –
my three sons, my three Oscars.
Notice my dignified eyes,
the nobility in my features,
my youth,
beauty,
speed,
my power,
each gift in triplicate.
I'm a triad of young men,
action-ready and able,
and yet,
I'm triplet virgins also
in love with three young men –
virile volatile virgins,
snared under the budding shadows
of the trees' strange shades –
the swan, the raven, the thrush
wrestling in my mind.
Don't you see the young men
with the maidens
chatting, giggling
and warbling tunes
walking hand-in -hand
on this endless, endless
boreen,
where gold glisters
all around them?'

Ciaran Carson

The Indian Mutiny

There I was
looking down the muzzle
of a hostile gun

with a spyglass –
I think, said I, they're
going to fire at us,

and as I spoke, *pluff*
came a spurt of smoke
with a red tongue in it –

a second of
suspense, when *whi-s-s-h*, right
for us came the round-shot

within a foot
of our heads, and plumped
into the ground a storm

of dust and grit
with which we upped and away
and into the courtyard.

No-one asked us
for our passes
as we climbed the staircase

to the upper room through
heaps of glass and broken mirrors,
tapestries and beds of silk,

to stare into the blue beyond
of palaces and azure minarets,
domes, temples, colonnades

and long façades
of fair perspective. Look for miles
away, and still

the ocean spreads,
the towers of the city
gleam amidst it,

spires of gold
and constellated spheres
so bright

I had to rub my eyes
before this vision
vaster and more beautiful

than Paris; down
another staircase then,
into a courtyard

large as Temple Gardens
bounded by a range of palaces
of gilt and stucco:

green shutters
and Venetian blinds occlude
the apertures which pierce

the walls in double rows,
and there are statues, fountains,
orange-groves, aqueducts

and kiosks, burnished domes
of metal, fresco paintings
on the blind-windows.

Through all these
the soldiery run riot,
forcing their way

into the long corridors –
you hear the crack
of musketry, the crash

of glass, as little jets
of smoke curl out from
the closed lattices.

The orange-groves
are strewn with dead
and dying sepoys,

the white statues
drenched with red.
Against a smiling Venus

a British soldier shot
through the neck
pumps gouts of blood

and soldiers drunk
with plunder pour out
from the broken portals

bearing china vases,
teapots, lamp-shades, mirrors,
which they dash to pieces,

others busy gouging
the precious stones
from stems of pipes,

from saddle-cloths, from
hilts of swords, from pistol-butts,
their bodies swathed

in gem-encrusted stuffs:
court after court
connected by arched passageways

where lie the dead sepoys,
clothes smouldering
on their flesh.

One who had his brains
dashed out by round-shot
made me think –

minutes telescoped
into each other – twelve inches
lower and I'd not

be here to write
nor would you read
this news of how

we freed Lucknow.

Ann Galvin

Inside and Outside

Outside there is a hill
Inside a valley
And a swan
And a golden nugget

Inside there is a fear
Outside its daughter
Among the trees
Glistening

Come here daughter
See what's in my hand
Our twined hearts
For cutting

These are the moments
We will treasure

Look inside your navel
You should find a clue
A book of proverbs
Or a map

The goldminers will be coming
With their black hands
They will want
To touch you

Their footprints will cover
The valley but their lamps
Will be extinguished
Like dinosaurs

Listen daughter
To the lapping
Of inside against outside
Outside against in

Everything else
Will be swept away

Gerard Smyth

Hopkins

Wearing the blackest black
he arrived with a deep nostalgia
for the music of Henry Purcell.

It was a kind of banishment
being sent to that other isle:
tea and bread in the cold Jansenist house,
wet days of summer

in the garrison town beyond the Curragh.
A place to languish,
to listen to horse-traffic
or silence in the noonday chapel.

He arrived from somewhere far,
perhaps where the South Sea seemed to hang
or the wind of the valley
was dyed in the Blood of the Lamb.

Gerard Smyth

Portobello Bridge

Twice a day I carry my soul over water.
The seedy canal blackened by car exhaust.
When first I came to the footbridge
at the lock, as a child
with fishing net and pinkeen pot,
it was through Little Jerusalem:
the avenues of exile,
past the synagogue that is now the mosque.

On the long road with dome
and campanile, steps to the doors
and life above the shops,
the town clock faces four ways at once,
chimneys sprout weeds
and windows reveal
lodging-rooms with lanterns
of papier mâché.

Twice a day I cross the bridge
at Portobello; look to the hills
or leave them behind
in their morning glory beyond Rathmines.

Pickings And Choosings
– Dennis O'Driscoll selects further pronouncements on poets and poetry

"Most of us would go a long way to avoid the company of poets. They're at best disagreeable, and at worst repulsive. Selfish, testy, irresponsible, humourless, swollen-headed, and infinite liars, they're like crazy aunts or men with stains on their trousers who think it's funny to swear. Most of them seem to have spent too much time in the sun or locked up in high rooms, disappointed not to have been born Milton, stewing in their own considerable juices."
– Ian Sansom, *The Guardian*, 2 March 2002

"The cultural dynamism of any community is probably in inverse relationship to the number of self styled 'poets' it contains. The more the 'poets', the lower the overall cultural values, the less demanding the criticism, the less rigorous the personal discipline, the greater the self-indulgence, and worst of all, the more insufferably boring the society will be."
– Kevin Myers, *The Irish Times*, 2 April 2002

"The ethic we should associate with poetry – a lack of egotism; a painful sympathy for the common plight of common humanity; revulsion at the human cost of commerce; a concern, negatively or positively, with the spiritual – is difficult to reconcile with the competitive urge to best one's contemporaries, to carry off the glittering prizes, and to concentrate so much acclaim on one's own figure that shadows fall across all else."
– Robert Potts, *New Statesman*, 1 April 2002

"Poetry is about the intensity at the centre of life, and about intricacy of expression. Without any appreciation of those, people are condemned to simplistic emotions and crude expressions."
– Anne Rouse, *The Sunday Times*, 28 January 2001

"Poetry is a way of communicating a vast array of thoughts and feelings by concentrating them into minimal, or even single, points which describe the whole."
– Frieda Hughes, *The Guardian*, 3 October 2001

"Poetry discloses something that lies not so much in its words themselves as in what we see above and through them, in an experience that is more than purely verbal."
– David Gervais, *PN Review*, May / June 2002

"Taken on its own, in the abstract, the word 'poetry' is both radiant and resistant. It means so many things to so many people that it is more the signal of a value than a precisely determined lexical entity."
– Seamus Heaney, *The European English Messenger*, Autumn 2001

"A poem without internal contradiction is not a poem."
– Donald Hall, *American Poetry Review*, January / February 2002

"A poem that does its work must stand on the knife edge of yes and no. The last line of a poem should have both the yes and the no in it; that's what makes it complex."
– Dorianne Laux, *Kansas City Star*, 28 January 2001

"Poetry is a kind of multi-faceted reaction to what goes on in your head. It's not a reasoned, serious attempt to understand things. It's play."
– Peter Porter, *The Age*, 14 May 2001

"Writing is a way not just of ordering and making sense of our experience, but actually a means of opening ourselves to experience."
– Peter Sansom, *Contemporary Poems*, 2000

"Poetry connects us to what is deepest in ourselves. It gives us access to our own feelings, which are often shadowy, and engages us in the art of making meaning. It widens the space of our inner lives. It is a magical, mysterious, inexplicable (though not incomprehensible) event in language."
– Edward Hirsch, *The Washington Post*, 13 January 2002

"Poetry might be roughly defined as the most exact and concentrated way of reflecting human experience in words – experience at its fullest being a complex of intellectual, imaginative, emotional and sensory perceptions."
– Richard Kell, *Other Poetry*, No. 17, 2000

"Writing poetry looks simpler than playing the fiddle. But it requires the same amount of skill. Picking up a violin doesn't make you a fiddler, yet people with a pencil and paper can easily believe they are poets."
– Don Paterson, *The Sunday Times*, 28 January 2001

"That which fleets by has great significance. The most delicate things are the ones that in the end prove strongest."
– Seamus Heaney, *Chicago Tribune*, 3 June 2001

"Good poems are flashes of light in the darkness of the heart and mind."
– Brendan Kennelly, *Irish Independent*, 7 April 2001

"I believe very strongly that a poem should be a disturbing unit; that, when one goes into that force field, one will come out the other end a changed person."
– Paul Muldoon, *BBC Radio 4*, 2001

"A poem is an interruption of silence, whereas prose is a continuation of noise."
– Billy Collins, *The Paris Review*, Fall 2001

"Every real poem is the breaking of an existing silence, and the first question we might ask any poem is, What kind of voice is breaking silence, and what kind of silence is being broken?"
– Adrienne Rich, quoted in *San Francisco Chronicle*, 27 May 2001

"Poetry tends to like blind spots; it so often burrows where it really oughtn't to, or delves past decency and approbation."
– Vona Groarke, *The Dublin Review*, Winter 2001/2

"Line is the poem's fundamental limit and law. It marks the edge of possibility and permitted extension."
– Karen Volkman, *Fence*, Fall / Winter 2000/1

"Form is part of the content, not its container; an interpretive pattern, not a stay against confusion; a process of invention, not the pediment of experience."
– J.C.C. Mays, *The Dublin Review*, Spring 2002

"A poem can include a statement but a poem can't be a mere statement."
– Pat Boran, *The Stinging Fly*, Spring / Summer 2002

"What one should write about is an important question for a poet, but it is separate from the question of what *moves* a poet to write."
– Robert B. Shaw, *Poetry*, February 2001

"Even before it is ready to change into language, a poem may begin to assert its buried life in the mind with wordless surges of rhythm and counter-rhythm. Gradually the rhythms attach themselves to objects and feelings."
– Stanley Kunitz, quoted in *Poetry London*, Spring 2002

"When I can't write poetry, which I find difficult, I write prose. I find I write poetry uphill and write prose downhill."
– Dannie Abse, *The Guardian*, 29 September 2001

"Poet-critic: there is a temptation to read the hyphen as a subtraction sign, as if every brainwave of the latter robbed the world of the former's next villanelle or sestina."
– David Wheatley, *The Dublin Review*, Spring 2002

"Who hasn't felt that subtle, sometimes violent shift in estimation upon seeing a poet repeat himself? If the greatest sin is being boring, then surely a close second is dulling some past excitement by revisiting it again and again."
– Peter Richards, *Verse*, Vol.17, Nos. 2 & 3, 2001

"A major poet does something slightly beyond the possible. When you read a minor poet, you're not necessarily reminded of someone else…yet you're always reminded that someone else is better."
– William Logan, *Parnassus*, Vol.25, Nos. 1 & 2

"At many literary journals, the editors typically receive only one work of criticism for every one hundred creative works."
– D.W. Fenza, *The Writer's Chronicle*, February 2001

"Some poets, doves by temperament, are not suited to criticism. But many are simply too fearful…If reviewers, like a chorus of Pollyannas, hail nearly every poet as being worthy of a laurel wreath, why should we believe them?"
– Herbert Leibowitz, *Parnassus*, Vol.25, Nos. 1 & 2

"One hesitates to review slim vols these days – the poetry world seems to be getting tighter all the time, what with that frightening near-parity of audience and practice (everyone who reads the stuff seems to write it, too), and that in-depth familiarity that poetry critics tend to have for their subject."
– Nicholas Lezard, *The Guardian*, 31 March 2001

"The real work of poetry has almost always occurred outside of whatever inner circle of ordained poets and critics happens to hold sway at the moment."
– Christian Wiman, *Poetry*, May 2001

"Anthologies are usually masquerades in which partiality is presented as comprehensiveness, individual taste or prejudice as historical objectivity and close personal friends as the future hopes of poetry."
– David Kennedy, *PN Review*, September / October 2001

"Beyond hype, flak, sectarian drivellings and glum jealousies, poetry remains to be read and heard."
– Sean O'Brien, *PBS Bulletin*, Spring 2001

"There's no question that there's more poetry sold now than there was thirty years ago. It's absolutely incontestable."
– Jonathan Galassi, *The Paris Review*, Summer 2000

"Production is outstripping demand, and the market cannot sustain this. Just as we need forests to mop up the excess carbon dioxide in the atmosphere, so we need new readers to absorb all this verse."
– Adam Newey, *New Statesman*, July 2001

"Poets are the second-class citizens of the literary world, which makes them roughly 12th class citizens of the media world."
– David Kipen, *San Francisco Chronicle*, 22 July 2001

"It might be true that the majority of people have little interest in, or don't know how to read, poetry but it is not for any poem to make concessions to that lack of curiosity or application."
– Greta Stoddart, Poetry*news*, Spring 2001

"All long poems – even *Paradise Lost*, even *The Prelude* – have moments when the reader can imagine the poet shambling in, muttering, 'I suppose I'd better write a few more lines of this thing' (for that is how long poems get written)."
– Neil Powell, *Times Literary Supplement*, 22 June 2001

"A lot of young poets these days are being educated into a state of hysterical aesthetic complexity. I saw poetry worksheets from the University of Iowa this year and what I saw was a widespread terror of not being smart, and a compensating effort to intimidate the reader."
– Tony Hoagland, *Fence*, Fall / Winter 2000/2001

"In the same way that each generation is taller, reaches puberty sooner, lives longer, and is more affluent than the previous ones, so does the impulse to write and publish poetry grow stronger, the need to attend creative writing workshops become more pressing."
– Joan Houlihan, *The Boston Comment*, 2001

"One of the troubles with all creative writing programs is the necessity to expose work to public scrutiny before it has had time to develop in privacy."
– Donald Hall, *American Poetry Review*, January / February 2002

"Poetry is a craft that one learns over a long period of time. But you only learn it if certain gifts are there to begin with – an imagination, the ability to make metaphor, a sense of language and rhythm and sound, intelligence, passion, curiosity, a great deal of empathy, and a fire in the belly."
– Stephen Dobyns, *Rattle*, Winter 2001

"Perhaps [the Arts Council] should follow the CAP model more closely and adopt a policy of set-aside: pay poets to lie fallow for a few years. I can think of a few good candidates for this."
– Adam Newey, *New Statesman*, July 2001

"Only publish what you know is as good as it can ever be, allowing always for a sort of private footnote that it's still not good enough. Then you might be getting somewhere toward the correct view of how to live as a poet."
– Ian Hamilton, *London Review of Books*, 21 February 2002

"The tiny oeuvre is a courtesy to the reader and a bribe to posterity."
– Don Paterson, *Oxford Poetry*, Summer 2001

"Two or three lyrics can make a poet immortal, but to build a readership during your lifetime – especially these days, when the media-saturated collective memory is so short – it is wise to be steadily productive."
– John Kerrigan, *Metre* 9, 2001

"Satire is a mode little practised nowadays, at least in American poetry. The kinds of savage attacks poets turned on their rivals in the eighteenth century are understandably out of fashion in a world where you never know who's going to be on the next grant panel or prize committee."
– Vernon Shetley, *Metre* 10, 2001

"It is absolutely amazing how many great poets started as seemingly talentless half-wits."
– Charles Simic, *New York Review of Books*, 12 April 2001

"A poet's talents exist in productive tension for only a decade or so. Before, the language is all main force, the subjects mistaken, the voice immature; after, the poet often hardens into manner, his subjects written to extinction."
– William Logan, *The New Criterion*, June 2001

"We forget how rarely a poet of substantial early achievement 'develops', as well as how common it is to have simply a decade or so of real originality over the course of one's life. That we can't know this about ourselves is...a kind of grace."
– Christian Wiman, *Poetry*, November 2001

"When you rhyme, you're somehow engaging with something that's older than you are, that's older than your history, that's older than anything you really understand or experience. You engage with a source of power; you're plugging into Dante, plugging into Coleridge."
– Glyn Maxwell, *Atlantic Unbound*, 14 June 2001

"Writing poetry gives you energy. There is a great restoration of yourself spiritually after writing a poem."
– Elaine Feinstein, *BBC Radio 4*, October 2001

"There is a certain kind of poet who is a clerk during the day. It seems to be necessary to have mundaneness, which must involve paperwork, the long, slow soporific afternoons at an office, the sedateness of security, a regular paycheck…"
– Rachel Cohen, *The Threepenny Review*, Winter 2002

"For a chap with a face like a butternut squash, the voice of a clinically depressed I-Speak-Your-Weight machine, the *joie de vivre* of a Southend clam and the swashbuckling sex appeal of Lord Irvine of Lairg, the late Philip Larkin still manages to generate excitement."
– John Walsh, *The Independent*, 24 April 2001

"Much of Robert Burns's thinking was done below the neckline, and a good deal of it below the waist."
– Ian McIntyre, *The Times*, 14 November 2001

"A good erotic poem will express desire; incite desire."
– Smita Agarwal, *Poetry Review*, Winter 2000/1

"Most poems in translation are affairs. With novels, I suspect, it's more like a marriage."
– Seamus Heaney, *The Paris Review*, Summer 2000

"Love these days usually comes dressed in inverted commas."
– Sue Hubbard, *Poetry London*, Spring 2001

"Poets make notoriously dicey lovers, prone as they are to fusty classical allusions, a documentary impulse in the bedroom, ego, overweening love of nature and – in the case of middle-aged male poets – the hazardous tutoring of young female students."
– Emily Nussbaum, *New York Times*, 30 December 2001

"Given a poetic landscape greatly influenced by the workshop, it is not surprising that many contemporary poems wind up paralyzed by their literalness: confessional narratives with allegiance to facts over aesthetics, metaphors that fail to transcend."
– Pamela Greenberg, *Harvard Review*, Spring 2001

"The poets' monopoly on confessional outpourings has been usurped by Oprah and her ilk. Poets have lost something of their primal function."
– Michael Wright, *The Sunday Times*, 28 January 2001

"It's finally impossible to consider fully any poet's body of work without considering his or her character, with how it determined the work, and then with how the work may in turn have affected the poet."
– C.K. Williams, *Yale Review*, October 2000

"You don't read poetry to find out about the poet, you read poetry to find out about yourself."
– Billy Collins, *The Globe and Mail*, 15 September 2001

"Some poems, like some people, have a certain charm; it would be interesting to research one day whether the two, poetic charm and personal charm, are inter-related."
– Carol Rumens, Poetry*news*, Summer 2001

"The extent to which we are all (except a very few saints among us?) influenced in our appreciation of contemporary writing by knowledge of the personal history and personal manner and personal affinities and even personal appearance of a given author is a subject more complicated and interesting (and embarrassing) than most of us admit."
– Mark Halliday, *Poetry Review*, Autumn 2001

"One reason readers prefer biographies of poets to their poetry is that the lives are more poetic, and more unlikely, than the poems."
– William Logan, *Parnassus*, Vol.25, Nos. 1 & 2

"There has to be a line between my life and art. You don't want to sell the one as the other…I don't simply want to tell what is. I want to tell what is with all the radiations around it of what could be."
– Anne Carson, *Poets & Writers*, March / April 2001

"It's a bad idea and a complete waste of time to prescribe what poets must or must not do because the best ones will always rebel and do the opposite."
– Charles Simic, *New York Review of Books*, December 2001

"It took time for me to understand that everybody, in the end, generates his or her own ecosystem as a writer. And, if you don't, nobody else is going to give it to you."
– Eavan Boland, *The New Yorker On-Line*, 26 October 2001

"Poetry is meant to be difficult like any interesting and enduring art form. If people want their art to be like a pop song with a hook then they should look elsewhere."
– Robin Robertson, *The Globe and Mail*, 2 February 2002

"Poetry is a poor tool for accurate observation; language drives toward abstraction, and in spite of itself makes what is seen into a symbol."
– Adam Kirsch, *The New Republic*, 29 August 2001

"It's hard to trust a poet who isn't, at least on occasion, a little bit funny."
– Dwight Garner, *New York Times*, 23 September 2001

"Poetry is one of the original grief counselling centres."
– Billy Collins, *The Globe and Mail*, 15 September 2001

"The picture (shows) the face of a young doctor who used to read poetry before he became a terrorist leader."
– Report from Afghanistan, *The Sunday Times*, 14 October 2001

"Radovan Karadzic is said to be…concentrating on poetry – a favourite pastime."
– Tom Walker, *The Sunday Times*, 14 October 2001

"I have now decided to continue with my war poetry until all the injustices in the world have been resolved."
– Ben Okri, *The Daily Telegraph*, 2 February 2002

"The trouble with most political poetry is that it is self-deluding."
– Helen Vendler, *New York Review of Books*, 31 May 2001

"He admired action-man/woman politics. Mrs Thatcher was a big enthusiasm. Michael Heseltine became a friend. Kenneth Baker – Thatcher's ideologue-in-chief – was also a buddy. He liked Mrs T's belligerent business sense, her militarism, patriotism and all-round impatience with slackers. These were traits he shared and was proud of."
– Horatio Morpurgo, on Ted Hughes, *Areté*, Autumn 2001

"I don't think poetry is gendered…but I think the politics of poetry are gendered."
– Paula Meehan, *Lyric FM*, January 2002

"Poetry long-term needs disinterested devotion. Women are better at this."
– U. A. Fanthorpe, Poetry*news*, Summer 2001

"John Basinger has memorized the entire text of Milton's narrative poem, 'Paradise Lost'...All 12 books, all 10,565 lines, all 100,000 words (give or take)."
– Deborah Hornblow, *The Hartford Courant*, 7 December 2001

"It is interesting and exciting that, as poetry once more becomes a performance art, women poets are now far more successful than they were, for instance, in the mid-twentieth century when the density of interlocking and abstruse allusions was the true note by which to know a poet."
– Germaine Greer, *The Observer*, 4 November 2001

"For the 'audience', listening to poets, rather than reading poems, prevents a full experience of the complexity, the substance, the music of verse. The poem is always only what the poet wrote down on the page. Everything else is show business."
– Adam Kirsch, *Slate*, 4 December 2001

"When people read poetry out loud...they always use a version of the poetry voice. It's that slightly reverential voice, slightly slowed down from real life, slightly too ponderous to get the rhythms going...The only good thing about the Poetry Voice is that it lets you know that what is being read is meant to be poetry, and nowadays it is not always easy to tell."
– Miles Kington, *The Independent*, 4 October 2001

"A poet's first duty isn't to explicate but to sing."
– Brad Leithauser, *New York Times*, 22 July 2001

"The late John Hewitt was the Leonard Cohen of Belfast. Happily the pub/restaurant named after him has completely missed the point and serves up cheerful dishes in a bright and breezy atmosphere."
– Matthew Fort, *The Guardian*, 20 April 2001

David Wheatley

Get Orf Moy Laaand!

Keith Tuma (ed.), *Anthology of Twentieth-Century British and Irish Poetry*, Oxford University Press, stg£65.99 hb., stg£29.99 pb.

Keith Tuma is American. This is worth pointing out straight away, since we don't take kindly in these parts to outsiders telling us what to think of ourselves. Maybe it's been the spectacle of Hugh Kenner down the years, ticking off the Irish for their failure to salute the genius of Desmond Egan and the Brits for just about everything since Basil Bunting, but Americans offering us a quick fix of modernism can be fairly sure of a glacial response. As Farmer Palmer's rifle-toting son Jethro in *Viz* might say: 'Get orf moy laaand!' And sure enough, when Tuma's *Anthology of Twentieth-Century British and Irish Poetry* arrived last year, hostilities didn't take long to break out. Reviewing the book in *Poetry Review*, Sean O'Brien diagnosed a bad case of post-imaginative, culturally imperialist cack. Glibly obfuscating tin-eared no-hopers, added David Harsent.

Let's give them credit for frankness, at least. There is plenty in this anthology that will surprise, baffle and infuriate, but when I think of menaces to British and Irish poetry today, Keith Tuma comes fairly low down the list. Fairly low, that is, in comparison to the spectacle of John Carey asking Maeve Brennan, apropos of Philip Larkin, What was he like as a lover? in *The Sunday Times*; to descriptions of *Birthday Letters* as Ted Hughes's greatest book; or to a poetry primer forcing the Prozac down with a reassurance that contemporary poetry is not that difficult, not elitist, obscure or irrelevant, and it's written for you...to take only three random examples. If the average Poetry Book Society member does fancy losing a night's sleep, then let it be over something more earth-shattering than Keith Tuma's preference for Cris Creek and Geraldine Monk over Glyn Maxwell and Simon Armitage.

If nothing else, the hostile noises this book has elicited might make people think again about the shabby, anthology culture we live in. Today's standard-issue anthology poem will be one or two pages long, or in exceptional circumstances three. It will hug the left-hand margin and divide into stanzas, with the option of a form of terminal consonance otherwise known as rhyme down the right-hand side. It will deal with a striking episode from the author's experience, perhaps in a spirit of playful irony (if the poem is by Carol Ann Duffy it may also feature some use of persona). At a pinch it will encourage us to rethink our views on race, identity and gender.

This is all very unfair, I admit. I enjoy the well-made lyric as much as the next reader, but there comes a time when even the most fatalistic devotee of the anthology-sized poem needs something different. As Justin Quinn pointed out to readers of *Poetry Review* recently, reminding them why they need to read Thomas Kinsella: there are worlds of emotion and intellect beyond *The Whitsun Weddings*, which is not to say that Larkin's work is second-best – it is the best of its kind, but there are other types of excellence. And so despite its multiple sins, of omission and commission, I was all for Tuma having a go and wrenching British and Irish poetry free of its usual bearings.

Reading through the book, I found myself compiling a list of antidote poetry, antidotes to the usual conventions and spatial limits of anthology culture. Here are some: Hugh McDiarmid's *A Drunk Man Looks at the Thistle*, David Jones's *The Anathemata*, Mina Loy's 'Songs to Joannes', W. S. Graham's *The Nightfishing*, Roy Fisher's *City*, Thomas Kinsella's 'Peppercanister' sequence, Geoffrey Hill's 'The Mystery of the Charity of Charles Péguy', Douglas Oliver's *Penniless Politics*, David Constantine's *Caspar Hauser*, Peter Reading's *C*, Randolph Healy's '*Arbor Vitae*', Eiléan Ní Chuilleanáin's 'Site of Ambush', Kathleen Jamie's *The Autonomous Region*, Peter Sirr's 'A Journal' and Alice Oswald's *Dart*. Some of these make it into Tuma's book, along with plenty of other rough beasts normally confirmed strangers to the anthologist's art. Some of these were real discoveries: I'd certainly never come across Lynette Roberts, the one and only Latino-Welsh modernist, and her long Second World War poem 'Gods with Stainless Ears'. Other figures like John Rodker and Clere Parsons strike me as historical curiosities destined to remain just that.

But it's the post-1945 section that readers are going to have most fun with. Anyone unfamiliar with the poets of Crozier and Longville's anthology *A Various Art* may be more than a little surprised at how few of these contemporary poets they recognise. And conversely, the more hard-line experimenter may feel Tuma shows strong deviationist tendencies by letting token mainstreamers like Shapcott, Duffy and Lochhead in (though far fewer mainstream men).

It is possible to cling too jealously to water-tight divisions of contemporary poetry into mainstream and other, as some of the other poets have done since the prelapsarian days of Eric Mottram at *Poetry Review*. The presence of Lee Harwood, Andrew Duncan and Michael Haslam in the first *Poetry Review* of the new Potts/Herd administration is a useful breaching of walls; you never know where it might happen next. What was the word Beckett used to describe MacGreevy? Not modernist but independent. Independents are what we need today.

One final illustration of the truth that big, baggy awkward poems really can bypass the arbiters of today's soft-centre/prize-poem/anthology culture. Watching Sky News once I saw what I'd hazard a bet was the only poetry-based item ever in the history of that channel. A performance was taking place of the Kyrgyzstan national epic, the *Manas*, which is over half a million lines long and takes a month to recite, with the added excitement that the bards had decided to do so on horseback. British and Irish poets: forget the 'New Gen', forget winning the T.S. Eliot or Forward Prize, now you know what to do to get on cable TV!

Alex Davis

The Native Strain

Keith Tuma (ed.), *Anthology of Twentieth-Century British and Irish Poetry*, Oxford University Press, stg£65.99 hb., stg£29.99 pb.

One of the dedicatees of the *Oxford Anthology of Twentieth-Century British and Irish Poetry* is the late English poet-critic, Donald Davie, saluted by the anthology's editor, Keith Tuma, as one of the 'agents of transatlantic dialogue in poetry.' In a 1977 interview with Dana Gioia, Davie had contested those poets and critics who maintained that such 'dialogue' was irrelevant to an understanding and practice of English poetry at that date. There are those, he said, who cleave to a 'native tradition' in modern English poetry, traceable to Hardy, which survived the 'modernist revolution,' and which can be 'propped up' by pointing to the example of Philip Larkin and others. Belief in this native strain, however, is dangerous to English poetry, argued Davie, because it encourages the English 'to think that in some way they have been comfortably insulated from what we think of as the modernist revolution not just in poetry but in all the arts, indeed in the sensibility and the technology and the rest. It *cannot* be true that England is left out.' Davie's urgency is fuelled not by the rhetoric of polemic, but by the insistence that English poetry written in the wake of modernism *necessarily* bears the imprint of early twentieth-century experiments in the verbal, visual and other arts. Such a 'revolution' in the arts is part and parcel of the social changes brought about by the rapid strides in technology made in the second industrial revolution, and the mind-bending conclusions reached in the physical sciences in these same years.

Tuma's anthology might be read in the spirit of Davie's comments: as a compendium of British and Irish poets whose work either registers the impact of modernism *and* modernisation or is written in its far-reaching afterburn. Thus, that which Tuma's Preface labels British and Irish poetry's 'contributions to modernism' can take many forms beside a wish to imbibe and emulate the radical possibilities for poetry made possible by Americans like Pound and Eliot. True, many of the poets here represented – some of them rescued, for good or ill, from decades of neglect – are those for whom Pound's breaking of the pentameter proved irresistible. In the case of Basil Bunting, American objectivism was not the antithesis of Wordsworth, but its enabling complement. In the Irish context, the poets Thomas MacGreevy, Brian Coffey and Denis Devlin, owe as much to Eliot as they do to Joyce. But Tuma's anthology also provides examples of poets whose best work was often written out of an intensely ambivalent resistance to modernism: Austin Clarke – to take another Irish example – wrote his greatest poems, of which Tuma includes the metrical *tour de force* 'Forget me Not', out of an initially sceptical probing of the poetry of Pound and Eliot. Furthermore, this book reminds us that poetic innovation at the beginning of the century was not confined to Americans, expatriate or otherwise: the British poets Mina Loy and T. E. Hulme, both ably represented, were at the forefront of the European avant-garde. And while Hulme's involvement with early modernism is well known, it is salutary to recall the importance of Loy's astonishing poetic procedures on Pound's development as poet and theorist.

Given the generous bulk of this anthology, there are many neglected poems of the pre-War period off which Tuma blows the dust. Some are gems: Charles Madge's sequence 'Delusions', which puts into poetic form some of the work on Mass-Observation the poet was contemporaneously conducting, is incontestably a major poem of the 1930s. Likewise, the rhythmic variations achieved in Elizabeth Daryush's poems are among the more successful experiments in syllabic metre in the English language. And there are numerous such surprises. The editor's introductions to these lesser-known poets – as to the canonical figures – are concise and helpful, usefully providing further reading where available. Of even greater assistance are the footnotes, provided by Nate Dorward, which are well-nigh encyclopaedic in the wealth of data they provide.

Anthologies are contentious by nature as much as by design; their readers inevitably find omissions that grate. In the case of Tuma's, the anthology's representation of contemporary poetry has appeared, to some, as shockingly partisan. We find Trevor Joyce where we might expect Michael Longley, Geraldine Monk rather than Carol Rumens, and so on. But in this the anthology remains true to its editor's stated wish to extend his readers' sense of the diversity of British and Irish poetry by drawing attention to 'challenging or innovative work' from the last century. To that end, Tuma foregrounds at the anthology's close a number of contemporary poets who are actively engaged in something related to Davie's preferred transatlantic dialogue. Whether his choices are prescient or not is neither here nor there, for us at least. Did F. R. Leavis's slip over the merits of Bottrall invalidate the integrity of his search for new bearings in English poetry? Tuma's editorial principles, thankfully, are anything but Leavisite: rather, his selection is a cogent and refreshing intervention in the poetic dialogue in which so many of his poets are themselves interlocutors.

Alan Titley
The World In Irish

Cathal Ó Searcaigh, *Ag Tnúth leis an tSolas*, Cló Iar-Chonnachta, €15.24.
Gabriel Rosenstock, *Syójó*, Cló iar-Chonnachta, €7.
Paddy Bushe, *In Ainneoin na gCloch*, Coiscéim, €5.08.
Mícheál Ó Ruairc, *Loco i Lios na Caolbhaí*, Coiscéim, €5.08.

We never need reminding that poetry in the Irish language is in an exceptionally healthy state, modern and traditional in turn, lyrical and playful, pithy and rhetorical. Its only danger is that it will become a victim of its own success, and the continuing succession of books will drown out the memorable and the noteworthy. Despite a large number of fine general anthologies over the last ten or fifteen years, there is as yet no real critical or even readerly consensus as to what is great, good or indifferent. Unfortunately the ranking, and therefore the reception, of poets is often a matter of geography, or chance. Criticism lags way behind the production of poetry, and while this is an excellent thing, and how it should be now and forever, the lack of any kind of a *vade-mecum* remains a drawback for the general public.

Fortunately, Cathal Ó Searcaigh is recently beginning to get the kind of notice and readership that he deserves. *Ag Tnúth leis an tSolas: 1975–2000* is drawn from his seven previous collections, as well as providing new material. It is therefore a statement of his poetic standing. It allows the reader to trace the development of his art since his first collection a quarter of a century ago, as well as allowing you to wallow in a rich and enriching body of work. The development is not, of course, as valuable as the individual bits, but is nonetheless fascinating for lovers of poetry. There was always a tension between the Ó Searcaigh of the home place, and the Ó Searcaigh of the wider world. One senses at the beginning a young man wanting to get away and enjoy the great open spaces of life, whether in a big city or in the realms of his own capacious imagination. Here there is no Ó Direáinesque whining and pining about the awfulness of city life, and even where the poet finds the urban distasteful, he never plumps for the easy option of sentimentality. 'Miontragóid Chathrach' is one big statement of the fullness of life in London, capturing a moment in time and space almost like a documentary film or narrative, except that it is driven by his own sensibility. The world out there is a challenging place, full of excitement: there is no need to hug the shore.

However, this guy is a rooted wanderer, and by his third collection, *Súile Shuibhne* (1983), there is a sense in which the journey home has already begun. There was always a reverence for home, of course, but it was tempered by the need to explore as if driven by the belief that he who only knows Gort a'Choirce knows not Gort a'Choirce at all. 'Cor Úr' is, for example, an almost sexually explicit love poem to his own place, one which marks an acceptance that was always there in his love of language and of real quirky poetic people. The point is that there is no simple Cathal Ó Searcaigh. He can look to the wisdom of the older generation and lament the loss of local inspiration as in 'An Tobar', while praising Jack Kerouac and the Beats – the inspiration for the poet to travel his own road in love and freedom. He can write a lyric which seems out of the eighteenth century, and then drag out a long and lingering line like a piece of music. He has short sharp aphoristic poems knocking up against longer narratives – prose poems such as 'Lá de na Laethanta' and verses that could be sung. There are translations, versions and poems inspired by other poets from afar, demonstrating yet again that his life is dedicated to poetry and his muse. We are lucky that his verse play *Oíche Ghealaí i nGaililí* is included as well as that scary rough uncompromising narrative of abuse, 'Gort na gCnámh'.

Much has been made lately of the fact that Ó Searcaigh's love poetry is gay, and this is hugely important to him. This fact he has not hidden under a bushel. So while we cannot say that this is unimportant, as it plainly is of great significance to him, his love poems are first and foremost love poems between people. There is always the suspicion that a poet as prolific as Ó Searcaigh will begin to tail off and lose some of his poetic sources. There is no sign that this is going to happen. In recent years he has got inspiration from his journeys to Nepal and his 'Kathmandu' is a great prayer to a great mountain. Looking back to the beginning, we realise that the style was always there, the love of words, of diction, of the poetic turn, but now at the height of his powers we sense a confidence and drive which is entirely his own and not beholden to anyone.

In a poem called 'Agallamh', Gabriel Rosenstock interviews

himself and asks who his readers are. He answers that one of them is certainly the 'Guru of the mountains', that is, Cathal Ó Searcaigh, and the other is himself. He may be only a poet and one of God's fools. This could be a moment of self-doubt on Rosenstock's part, but is more likely a kind of playful comment on his own work. Even though he also wanders far and wide for his inspiration, his internal landscape is a very different place to Cathal Ó Searcaigh's. It is different because while Ó Searcaigh is always himself, Rosenstock is many people. Anything can happen in his poems, and indeed it does. 'An t-iarthraenálaí dreancaidí sorcais' is a typical Rosenstockian title (if anything can be typical), and glorifies the small and the insignificant; in contrast 'Xolotl' is a hymn to the big things in life: languages and words and gods.

It would be wrong to talk of his *drawing* inspiration from anywhere. His poems just seem to happen. He makes poetry out of a lift in 'Thuas seal, thíos seal', and it is both clever and wise. Saying goodbye to a pair of old spectacles is in that great Irish tradition of being able to make poetry out of anything at all. He tells stories, has fun, and coins 'new' old saws. His love of Zen 'learning' and practice appear intermittently, and it must always be said that he was the first of them all to internationalise poetry in Irish, meaning beyond the narrow confines of fortress Europe. As against that he can be as 'traditional' as us all in his homage to the great storyteller Seán Ó Conaill, or in his retake on the poems on Liadhain. Most importantly, Rosenstock is always a pleasure to read. Even when he deals with the horrors of Kosovo, where the world is turned upside down and pathetic fallacies are made new, his craft carries us along through the awfulness of it all. While it can hardly be said that Rosenstock is a neglected figure after his prodigious output of more than one hundred books of all kinds, the catholicity and generosity of his vision has often been underplayed. If he had stuck to one last rather than dozens, his remarkable poetry might have gained louder notice. But I don't think he would want a syllable of this collection changed. In it he has got his syójó working to full capacity.

Whether it is growing globalisation and ease of travel, or simply a coincidence, Paddy Bushe also takes us east. His 'Buachaillí Tibeiteacha', Tibetan boys, are like nothing in a poem by Cathal Ó

Searcaigh, but just fun-loving individuals; his Zen stories would certainly be attractive to Gabriel Rosenstock; and his Chinese verbs and sages testify to his own loving search for what is apt and precise and just right. He returns us to Europe, of course, with translations from Rilke and Celan, and we come right back home to the Kerry of Uíbh Ráthach in a series of poems celebrating the coming of the Irish to Ireland, at least according to the pseudo-historical *Book of Invasions*. They landed on the south Kerry coast, whereupon Aimhirgin composed and declaimed his great poem, supposedly the very first poetic utterance in Western Europe that has come down to us. Factual tosh, undoubtedly, but great for poetry. Paddy Bushe takes on the myth and reworks it in a series of poems that are learned, individual, highly wrought and powerful. They celebrate the tradition while examining, turning and undermining it. In finely-charged language they announce the permanence of rock and landscape against the wind of words. And yet his words are sharp and hard and cut. But for all their reverence he can rewrite Aimhirgin's poem in 'Leagan Eile', giving it a modern twist that is both humorous and sardonic.

But Bushe is also a poet of moments. 'Lagtrá' might be everybody's idea of what a certain kind of lyric poem should be, simple, moving and hauntingly atmospheric; while 'Paidir Oíche' is one of those deeply satisfying poems because the poet is at home with himself, happy for all those ordinary things of life and the way he is now. It is a poem which has a glow about it. Some of that same glow attends his 'Oileán Eile Fós', where Seán Ó Ríordáin's much-remembered wrestlings of conscience are replaced by a saner and quieter vision.

The Kerry connection is maintained by Mícheál Ó Ruairc, who has made the serious mistake of being funny, and even worse than that, being clever. Poetry is not meant to be funny, at least not as consistently as this. Being funny means you are not a proper poet and are not likely to stick your head in the oven. And it is because there aren't many like him that it is these quirky, unusual, slanted, off-beam poems that will be remembered, despite his hard, heartbreaking, loving pieces on the life and death of his parents which are a central part of the book. These are tender and sad and tragic and memorable, as the poem on his son is gentle and protective.

But for all that, the wild stuff will out. 'Faobhar' is almost like a personal manifesto, or so I imagine it. It tends towards rhetoric (and I mean this as praise), and you can almost hear the swish of a blade as it cuts through humbug and charlatanry. This hard carapace against the world is the opposite of his tender self, but it is also that which produces the humour and the jaundiced eye and the 'can't fool me' stand against all-comers. 'Dar fia!' is a hilarious account of an encounter of his car with a deer while driving through the Phoenix Park. He has fun with language, as he has fun with *dánta grá*, with critical theory, with teaching (through a certain amount of sardonic glances); and can be frighteningly perceptive as in 'An ráfla', pen-picturesquely in 'Radharcanna ón Spáinn'; or jeer wonderfully at the poetry of place and at places themselves in 'Cúis Gháire Chugainn!' Over the years, students learning Irish were overly fed with *seanfhocail* as if they were the very pith of the language itself. Ó Ruairc takes his revenge on the hegemony of the *seanfhocal* in a poem which rewrites the best and the worst of them with a kind of wrathful glee. Not everyone will thank him for this, of course; but I do, as I hope most of the readers of this fine book will.

Gerald Dawe

AudioLogue

Christopher Logue, *AudioLogue: A Seven CD Set of Recordings 1985–1998*, Unknown Public Ltd., stg£49.50.*

Christopher Logue is probably best know today for his versions of Homer's *Iliad*, published by Faber & Faber under the title *Kings*, *The Husbands* and *War Music*. But as his *Selected Poems* (Faber & Faber, 1996) makes plain, he has been sounding his own war music since just after World War II, casting cold and hot eyes on his fellow man and woman with echoes of a latter-day Blake. Logue's anger at the way the world wags is genuinely refreshing, even if it has been on the boil since the Fifties. What is also refreshing about Logue is the fact that he brought poetry and music together in the late Fifties and early Sixties and made the whole thing matter outside the heady confines of the seminar room or 'cultural event'.

In *AudioLogue*, the history of the various recordings which feature Logue are gathered for the first time into one compact box containing 500 minutes of words and music, along with a 24-page booklet with notes and commentary on the texts and recordings. Included are Logue reading *Kings*, *The Husbands* and *War Music*; reading his *Selected Poems*; *Red Bird*, the poems based on Pablo Neruda, recorded with the Tony Kinsey jazz quintet; *Loguerhythms*, the songs he wrote for Peter Cook's Establishment nightclub in the 1960s, sung by band and jazz singer, the immaculate Annie Ross; and *The Arrival of the Poet in the City*, a 20-minute musical setting by George Nicholson of Logue's text. This really is a most impressive collection.

As the late and lamented art critic and historian David Sylvester put it, reviewing a *Red Bird* gig for *The Observer* (when poetry readings were actually reviewed!): 'There was a lot of ingenuity and even more sheer beauty in this programme, surely one of the very few original contributions [England] has ever made to jazz, as well as one of the most civilized attempts to popularise poetry.'

The role of poetry as performance, and the value of poetry as song, may have left us all behind in the media-drenched marketing world of the 21st century. But Logue has fought for and found his own audience and space in contemporary culture, and his thoughts on these things matter: 'People will tell you,' he remarked in an interview with the Scottish writer James Campbell, 'that their education put them off poetry for life. It's complete nonsense. The truth is they had no taste for it and they are ashamed of that, so they blame the teachers.' Indeed, I should say that *AudioLogue* is perfect for any poetry teacher's classroom plans.

Christopher Logue's memoir, *Prince Charming* (Faber & Faber, 1999), was reissued last year by the same publisher in paperback, so alongside *AudioLogue* and the publication of the three Homer texts in a single volume, it's now possible to have the collected words of one of England's finest and most unique poetic voices available on this side of the pond.

*Available from: Unknown Public Ltd, Dept PUA, FREEPOST (RG 2558), Dept. WAL, PO Box 354, Reading RG1 5ZZ, United Kingdom.

Email: sales@unknownpublic.com

Michael S. Begnal

Comhthéacsanna Eile

Mícheál Ó Ruairc, *Loco i Lios na Caolbhaí*, Coiscéim, €5.08.
Máirín Nic Eoin (eagarthóir), *Gaolta Gairide*, Cois Life, €12.00.

The rural/urban dichotomy is a fairly long-standing one in Irish poetry of both languages, mirroring the dynamics of Irish society itself. The early pastoralism of Yeats set the precedent for much of what was to come later, while Kavanagh at least provided an unblinkered view of country life. Because of its material circumstances, Gaeltacht literature has often remained focused on rural matters, though giants in the field (such as Ó Riordáin, Ó Díreáin, etc.) never allowed themselves to be so restricted. Over the last several decades Irish society has become increasingly urbanized, and the Irish language and its literature has to a degree followed this trend.

The poet Mícheál Ó Ruairc reflects this sociological pattern, having been born and raised in Taobh a' Chnoic, Bréanainn, Leitriúch, Co. Kerry, but now living in Dublin for many years. Early in his latest collection, however, it becomes clear where his sympathies lie. 'Faobhar' is a forceful poem in which an old man, presumably from the poet's home place, extols the virtues and necessity of a blade:

> Tá an áit seo go léir ina fásach cheal faobhair:
> Faobhar na speile ag gearradh
> Sa mhóinéar um thráthnóna;
> Faobhar na scine ag lonradh
> Faoi sholas na gréine...

(This whole place gets overgrown without a blade: / The scythe's blade cutting the meadow in the afternoon; / The knife's blade shining / Under the light of the sun...)

And onward with a list of the different cutting tools needed to live in the proximity of, to control, nature. The city, on the other hand, does not fit into this scheme of things where the cosmos can be ordered with simple farm implements.

Dublin, for Ó Ruairc, is the triumph of chaos. It is a place where a row can inexplicably get out of hand in a Chinese restaurant, and you end up being threatened with a meat cleaver by the (racially-stereotyped) waiter:

> Agus maidir leis an bhfreastalaí starrfhiaclach fiarshúileach
> Déthónach ón tSín bhuel ba mhó ba chosúil le cearc
> I gcomhluadar sionnaigh é ná le ball den chine daonna...
> – 'Come Again!'

(And as for the buck-toothed slant-eyed double-arsed / Waiter from China, well he seemed much more like a hen / In the company of a fox than a member of the human race. . .)

Dublin is also the home of 'the Celtic Tiger', a worn-out phrase and played out concept which nevertheless becomes the target of Ó Ruairc's frustration in a couple of poems (along with mobile phones, his mortgage, and the Millennium). 'Tíogar Ceilteach 2000 A.D.' describes its subject in apocalyptic terms, and modern Ireland must seem like the end of the world as we know it, at least for a 'fear tuaithe' ('countryman', as the poet refers to himself in 'Aithne'). Ó Ruairc appears bewildered here as he paints a portrait of a sensibility wholly unsuited to an urban existence.

There is no real mediation in this collection. The speaker, the 'me', *is* the poet himself, the various complaints very much his own personal complaints. This is not to say that something similar wasn't going on in the work of a poet like Aodhagán O Rathaille, for example. But Ó Rathaille, with his language resources, is a tough act to follow. So a poem like 'Aoine 3:00 i.n.', in which Ó Ruairc whinges about his boring job as a schoolteacher, might be a useful release valve for the poet, but who really wants to read it without at least the consolation of some top-notch linguistic artistry...

> Mairim ó Luan go hAoine,
> Ó chupán caife go cupán caife,
> Ó bhriosca seacláide go briosca seáclaide,
> Ó chóipleabhar go cóipleabhar scoile.

(I live from Monday to Friday, / From cup of coffee to cup of coffee, / From chocolate biscuit to chocolate biscuit, / From copybook to school copybook.)

...it runs, boring the reader just as much as Ó Ruairc is bored by his life. Elsewhere he attempts levity – mainly in certain relationship poems – but often these verge on corniness. Fadlínte (`Meridians') is a case in point, where the poet, apparently straight-faced, utilizes the rather embarrassing phrase 'Dátlíne / Idirnáisiúnta / An Ghrá' ('the International Dateline of Love'). In 'Grá Geal' he promises his lover his last Rolo.

There is a certain responsibility attaching to a collection's title poem. Usually we expect it to sum up the volume's major themes, or at least stand out as one of the better poems in the book in question. Not so here. 'Loco i Lios na Caolbhaí' is a piece of fluff, a silly song complete with chorus, the endnote for which earnestly reminds us that *loco* means 'crazy' in Spanish.

In the wake of such poems comes 'Arraing ón Astráil', a telling piece written on receiving a rejection letter from an editor of an Australian literary magazine. You see this poem from time to time – the poet is stung by the rebuke of his work and writes a bitter put-down in reply. The thing is, in this case some of the nameless editor's comments ring true:

> "Ní hé nár gháireas,"
> Dúraís id litir dhiúltaithe,
> "Nuair a léas do dhánta...
> Ní hé, mhuis, nár gháireas
> ...
> Ach fós bhraitheas...fós bhraitheas,"
> Dúráis id litir dhiúltaithe,
> "Bhraitheas go raibh easnamh éigin orthu..."

("It's not that I didn't laugh," / You wrote in your rejection letter, / "When I read your poems... / It's not at all that I didn't laugh! [...] / But still, I felt...still felt," / You wrote in your rejection letter, / "I felt there was something missing in them. . .")

Is this not the sort of thing that might best be left out of the public domain if there's any chance at all that the reader could take the other side?

Before this review starts to look like a demolition job, which is not its intent, it should be stressed that there is some very good work here. The series of poems *in memoriam* of the poet's parents stand out as particularly accomplished. There is a gravity to these, often lacking elsewhere, which extends beyond the subject matter itself to Ó Ruairc's handling of it. Suddenly there is a quiet, brooding quality to the writing, capturing the strange sense of stillness that seems to descend over everything when someone dies:

> Tá Rí na farraige
> Ar lár anocht
> Ina luí sa reilig uaigneach.
> Tá Ríocht na bóchna
> Go dubhach
> Ag caoineadh
> I gucasa caola
> Agus ar chladagih thréigthe.
> – 'Caoineadh II'

(The King of the sea / Is missing tonight / Lying in the lonely graveyard. / The ocean Kingdom is / Gloomy / Keening . In narrow coves / And on abandoned beaches.

'Drochshúil' and 'Radharcanna ón Spáinn' are both noteworthy for their vivid scenes of death and gore, and their lack of sentimentality. 'Réamh-Dhán' and 'Iar-Dhán', the poetic siblings which bookend this collection, appeal for their mysterious image of a box floating down a river. The significance of the box remains uncertain, and it is tempting to call these surreal.

'Giobal' ('A Rag') is perhaps a more effective indictment of contemporary Ireland than Ó Ruairc's impotent jibes at the Celtic Tiger (again, one wishes to be done with this term). In the poem, the rag hangs there as a symbol of the Famine. Like an accusing ghost, it hangs

> mar bhrat cuimhneacháin
> ar an ngorta
> nach bhfuil ach scread asail uainn
> ar foluain
> taobh thiar dínn
> ar an líne
> sa chúlghairdín.

(as a cloth of remembrance / of the famine / which is but a donkey's scream away / floating / behind us / on the line / in the back garden.)

The phoniness, the shallow attitudes, the gross consumerism begotten by the recent economic boom will undoubtedly become even more objectionable as times get tougher once again. So it's not as if Ó Ruairc doesn't have good reason to bemoan the current state of affairs. Most of the time, however, he resembles a Lear raging vainly at forces he cannot control. The only alternative he seems able to offer is a sort of neo-pastoralism, as he returns again and again to his rural home for solace:

>   Taobh a' Chnoic
>   Áit a bhfuil doras ar leathadh,
>   Citeal ag fiuchadh romham
>   Ar an tine
>   Agus bord leagtha amach
>   Faoi mo choinne.
>   – 'Ceann Scríbe'

Taobh a' Chnoic / A place where a door is open / A kettle boiling before me / On the fire / And a table laid out / Waiting for me.)

Máirín Nic Eoin (the author of *B'Ait Leo Bean: gnéithe den idé-eolaíocht inscne i dtraidisiún liteartha na Gaeilge*, a study of gender ideology in Gaelic literature) has returned with an anthology of Irish-language poetry organized around the themes of youth and family relationships. Nic Eoin is a lecturer in Irish at Coláiste Phádraig, Drumcondra, and *Gaolta Gairide* derives from a course she teaches there on this type of literature.

The book collects work on this subject from a diverse range of contemporary poets, including such familiar names as Nuala Ní Dhomhnaill, Máire Mhac an tSaoi, Biddy Jenkinson, Michael Davitt, Áine Ní Ghlinn, Cathal Ó Searcaigh, and others. With one exception, all of these poems have appeared elsewhere, some in other anthologies, but it is the particular context that justifies their republication.

The only previously unpublished piece here is Máire Mhac an tSaoi's

'Do Mhaoilre', best described as a welcoming for a newborn grandchild. It rolls along with the rhetorical cadence of some ancient bardic poem as it celebrates the ever-miraculous coming of a new life, simple but eternal:

> Éadromaíonn an croí ionam
> Ar theacht duit ar an láthair,
> Is cuirim fad mo ghuí leat
> Trí phóirsí an lae amáirigh

(The heart lightens in me / When you are present, / And I put all my hope in you / Through the passages of tomorrow.)

Ní Dhomhnaill's 'An Bhatráil' is not at all simple, dealing as it does with the strong negative emotional forces a mother is sometimes subject to after the birth of her child. In the poem these forces are described in supernatural terms, deemed to be the work of the fairies. Yet at the same time it's but a metaphor, as the reader is given to know that this darkness might really come from inside the mother herself:

> Mar atá
> beidh mo leordhóthain dalladh agam
> ag iarraidh a chur in iúl dóibh
> nach mise a thug an bhatráil dheireanach seo dó.

(As it is / I'll have a hell of a time / trying to explain to them / that it wasn't me who gave him that last battering.)

Editor Máirín Nic Eoin earns kudos for steering away from the sappy, sentimental poetry that often appears in English-language anthologies on the subject. She notes this herself in her well-conceived introduction, singling out such books as *Mothers: Memories from Famous Daughters* and the recent *Talking of Mothers: Poems for Every Mother* as the sort of idealized view of motherhood she was trying to avoid. It's hard to imagine a poem on the order of 'An Bhatráil' appearing in such a book, or indeed any of the others that deal with the difficulties of the parent-child relationship (like Caitlín Maude's 'Oedipus Rex'). Colm Breathnach's tragic-comedic 'Oíche Mhaith, a Bhastaird' is a good example of how it's done from a male perspective.

Nic Eoin's introduction also places her topic in an historical context, reaching back to the Middle Ages for early examples from the Gaelic literary tradition, and to conventions of medieval literature from the European continent. The earliest poem to appear in *Gaolta Gairide* is Pádraig Ó hÉigeartaigh's 'Ochón! A Dhonncha' (lamenting the death of a son), first published in 1906. Interestingly, Seán Ó Tuama and Thomas Kinsella included this one in *An Duanaire* as 'a moving end to the high literary tradition of three centuries'. Here it is the start of something else.

This volume is a testament to the richness of contemporary Irish-language poetry and its ability to seek out new situations for itself in an ever-changing world. While *Gaolta Gairide* is restricted to a particular theme, it is obvious that Nic Eoin has a wealth of material from which to draw. In fact there are many other poets – Louis de Paor comes to mind – who could easily also have been included. No doubt such an absence is due to concerns of space, but at 95 pages perhaps there was room for more. The only other drawback to this anthology again concerns its restriction. The reader who does not have a particular interest in this subject, or who wishes for a more general overview of modern Gaeilge poets, may be better served by looking somewhere else.

The letter beginning on the opposite page was written to me by Paul Durcan when, as one can see by the date, both of us were young and enthusiastic poets. It has lain buried away in the archive of New Writers' Press all these years, surviving house-moves and the usual vicissitudes of daily living, and it surfaced only recently by chance. Re-reading it after all these years, I was struck by Paul's commitment to poetry as a deeply serious activity in the sense it is worth devoting a life to; and time has proved that.

Although we have gone our separate ways as Paul knew we inevitably would, we have both continued in our dedication to poetry. The value of what we have achieved is a matter for others to judge, and the publication of this letter is not intended to suggest that either of us feels he has reached a pinnacle of recognition or importance. Rather, it is intended to signal to young poets the kind of dedication that poetry will require of them if only to keep going in the hope, which is all it can be, that in time they may manage to write something worthwhile.

Placing the letter in this context, I asked Paul if he would allow me to publish it in *Poetry Ireland Review*. I wasn't sure what his reaction might be. He agreed on, the condition that I write this little note explaining why I thought the letter should be published, and making it clear that the idea of its publication was mine alone. I am happy to do that now.

Michael Smith, Editor

Paul Durcan

Letter from one Young Poet to Another

Friday, April 26, 1967

Michael,
Two men meet on a lonely road. They become great friends. They walk together for hours until the sun goes down below the nearest hill and the road forks. Each knows that his way is not the way of the other and so they shake hands, wish each other well and part. It is the same with poets. For each of us knows that our journey is ours and ours alone and ours to make alone. Though a blackbird must die bloodily, we must not curse a redwing's sniping at the greengage sun. Bless this signpost and set forth. We may or may not return to have our bloody feet washed by our maundy fathers in the dark. To be lustral in the arms of my girl is fine in all but now; lacerate the tongue & set forth.

It is hard. It is sometimes cruel. Now and then it is fatal. And yet it is required of those who wish to love and make love sing and echo in the trees and ages above the grave. Concerning the journey itself I cannot say nor wish even to hazard a forecast; only that it involves loneliness beyond the comprehension of those of us who think that we are lonely. I know that false tears cut no ice in sunlight.

I believe that each man kills the thing he loves *at present*. For whom the drum beats drives her blood to stone. But the possibilities are endless and the perspective timeless. We can and must wrap an horizon about her side and call to the heavens for whom the stars have ever tried to fall. Christ was the last of the Olympians and God is dead. How, then, can we be content to chatter and bubble above love in pubs and coffee-bars unto death.

> 'South,' Dara says. *South*.

The literary life of Dublin is blasphemy because it is cowardly, selfish and sometimes stupid. I have said that before. I never want to say it again. It is a broad generalisation. No doubt there are a few who are not cowardly, selfish & stupid. I believe that John Jordan is a noble person. I believe that X is a silly fop. That is just for the record: it is of no consequence in a way; in some ways it is important. The face of the earth is scarred from birth like mine. Do not forget I am one of the common centaurs too. Not, I hope, a whited sepulchre.

The greatest philosophers of our time were poets. Kierkegaard, Nietzsche, Heidegger. The greatest poets were philosophers. Hopkins, Eliot, Pound & Yeats, etc.. Gascoyne too. How do you decide between possibility and necessity, between the individual and the manifold, nothingness and existence? The poet is a man 'unhappily in love with God.'

If stones are to fall upwards then the individual *must* think himself to death. For the poet the concept is the image, the poem the invisible mirror of his being here at all or anywhere else. I cannot see how you, Michael, as a poet can avoid, still less ignore the oneiric kingdom where the nine-eyed man is jack.

> 'We Poets in our youth begin in gladness;
> But thereof come in the end despondency and madness.'

At the age of seven years & twenty-one days our youth ended. Cast out of the garden we must acknowledge anguish & madness, & accept these twin maidens of the dervish, and strangle them.

No longer can we be satisfied with 'gold curtains of rock hiding the bottomless sky'.

I personally accept Gascoyne's equations. Spirit with an awareness of possibility and Reason with the logic of necessity. It is out of the terrible conflict between these two maidens of the dervish that *The Poem* rises to the highest pitch of human love & hate.

The world today is one of formlessness. War, refugees, hunger, crime, suicide, birth-control, abortion, etc. The task of the poet is to find a form for formlessness. Again I would think that Gascoyne's statement and solution are good & indispensable for all of us. And it is here that you will come to see why poetry is apparently obscure and meaningless.

'The void itself cannot be apprehended except by means of symbolic expression... By realising such a term of reference we can free ourselves from the terrible non-existence implicit in the negation of the Spirit.'

Once you apprehend the void which is at the heart of out time then you will have left Ireland and gone south.

> 'And may we know thy perfect darkness
> And may we into hell descend with thee'.

Suffering, guilt, chance, conflict, death, all these are inescapable and no act is genuine unless it acknowledges and projects all five. These are the five fingers of the poet's hand. Evil, be thou my good, said Nietzsche.

Right now, I concentrate my being into all those endless possibilities of my existence. And the only one I desire is irretrievably closed to me. The gates are barred, the sentinel is almighty and profane. Yet I must break open the gates and tear the house down, brick by brick, till my loves are left naked in the dust of my sin. Outburst of eyes in the neap-tide pleasing with suns of the planet in the Fall that is my Spring. The neap-tide is perpetual.

That is why your words 'O feel the call before the fatal enmeshment' are, for me, futile. I am glad that you wrote them and I appreciate them. But I cannot 'welcome in your poet's life-spring'. Sin must be original for each of us; as must also be the way of the cross, the fourteen stations. The pyramid of blood in Egypt is here now in Ireland, not as a monument to Christ, but as a signpost to the people and to the poet. Though appeal to authority is the weakest argument of all, I cannot refrain from pointing to all the great writers of time. All took the same road, met at the same signpost, & parted. Homer & the Odyssey, Chaucer & Canterbury, Shakespeare & the canker in the rose...

If I may mention a practical difficulty, it is this: to do the right thing for the wrong reason is the greatest treason of all. This I fear terribly; it haunts me, at night especially.

> 'What images return / O my daughter.' She is dead.

And so I must unsheathe myself to the utter earth as the sword of a rose might saw the starfish through. Even an urchin may hope to live with his wife & child by the sea-faring tales of the tide & fishers of men.

Love,
Paul

David Lloyd

Chaos Theory

Randolph Healy, *Green 532: Selected Poems 1983-2000*, Salt Publishing, stg£ 8.95.

It is good to have this volume, a collection of poems previously published in small press editions and little magazines that are hard to come by. Randolph Healy is among the foremost of those who are currently engaged in Ireland in renewing and transforming the practice and possibilities of poetic language. I studiously avoid the expression 'an Irish poet', and not only because the community of Healy's readership, small as it may yet be, is one dispersed across the Anglophone world wherever poetic practice remains engaged with experiment. More significantly, Healy is a poet for whom the locutions of location are accidental. His work scrupulously avoids throughout the temptations of representation with its ample and amply evidenced rewards. *Green 532* (a note refers us not to flags or vegetal matter, but to the fact that green 'is the wavelength of light to which the human eye is most sensitive') contains no moral fables of Irish rural (or urban) life, no cute philologies of dialect, no trim quatrains that resolve the ethical dilemmas of the tribe. If Little Bray appears on the horizon, it is through the retina of sixty pigeons in flight, (as in 'BOIDS'), rather than as a synecdoche for the state of the nation, north or south.

The writing here eschews the well-made anecdotes by which the poem is elected to the curriculum, the mimetic adequacy that articulates the 'truth' of any given 'colony of belief', 'forgetting that precision/is only gained at a very low level/of meaning' ('Colonies of Belief'). To say this is to say more than that this work on its face even writes against possibly the most virtuous lure of representation, the condition by which the writer from a peripheral or minor culture nonetheless comes to express some universal intuitions. We have here, for all its greenness, a poetic that furthers the work of radically dismantling the aesthetic-political conjunctions that underwrite both the 'national-literary' and that to which it is a mere stepping stone, the universal. The very term that sustained that synecdochal relationship, voice, is dissolved in *Green 532*.

An active matrix of connections links the refusal of representation, the suspicion of singular voice and the recalcitrance of the poetry to an easy yield of consumable take-out meaning. Healy's poetry, in the slow release of its patterns and relations, is resistant to transparency, alert to the dangers of such readily portable consolations as all too much recent verse provides – 'over the chipper (another stabbing last week)/the respite centre, the short terraces...' ('BOIDS'). Its opacities demand the reader's restless engagement without the assurance that said reader will find somewhere at the putative core of the labyrinth the final figure of the poet.

If, from time to time and mostly out of the guarded and vulnerable intimacies of familiar life, a quotidian accent emerges, nothing signals that this is the stable centre of the work. Too many potentialities are ignited at once for any one system of language to subsume the others: 'And at any point it could have been different,/multiple branches and fibres fingering/every particle of the body of the possible.' ('Spirals Dance'). The resultant opacity of the poetry, which will doubtless infuriate some as wilful obscurity, dispossesses the subject of its integrity, casting it adrift in a sometimes manic ciphering.

Healy's is among contemporary work that ruptures a now two centuries old contract between reader and writer that still, still, haunts discussions of the poetic. When Wordsworth in 1800 declared that poetry was the language of man speaking to man, he mobilized an analogy with political society that was already suspect. Poetic like political representation sought to replace a radical conception of the commons, of a world in common, thereby displacing what it represented with a privileged and discrete domain of aesthetic commonality. Poetry, posed as a cure for the dissociative effects of the division of labour, as a site of transparent and equable representations of humanity in general, cannot escape the consequent conditions of its own specialization. Concealed in the apparent freedom of the Wordsworthian contract is the coercive clause that extracts the labour of the reader, subjected to the machinery of the poem. A whole disciplinary institution of aesthetic education has emerged from the contradictions of this contract without ever losing the illusion that its pedagogical function is to humanize its subjects. The ultimately academic rage against difficulty, or obscurity, in poetry betrays the anxiety that the continuing condition of its production is the very absence of communication. Healy seems to gesture towards something like this from the outset:

> M-A-N
> Spells
> And remains separate from
> Man.
> A boy is following him,
> Trying to keep in step.
> Success, then he begins to lag.
> And the difference increases
> Until he has to make a small
> Jump to get back in phase.
>
> .....
>
> Who saw a book?
> Who wanted to start from luminous statements
> And finally catch the world?
> Jump.
> The magnetic effect,
> The attraction which two rhythms have for one another.
> –'Poem in Spring'

However far we may believe we have moved beyond romanticism and its universalizing aesthetic claims, yet the debate that turns around the ethical demand for accessibility and transparency of poetic language – which guarantees its commonality – as against the no less ethical function of its difficulty and obscurity – which exacts the labour of human self-realization in the track of the poet – recurs to the same terms. Time and again, poetic revolutions are declared in the name of a reversion to the common language of men [sic], whether by Wordsworth or Pound, Williams or Olson, or in the colloquial energies of contemporary slam aesthetics. The ineluctable question remains deceptively obvious: whose voice? Not that that question should lead necessarily where it usually does, to an appeal for inclusion, for the embrace of prefabricated sub- or counter-cultural "voices". Such a move in fact merely replicates the notions of representation that underwrite aesthetic democracy and consigns us once again to the tired ruses of liberalism rather than moving the question and the practice on a little. What voice?

These contemporary questions have a longer history. The recurrent revisionary tendency is counterpointed by another (often in the same writer) that might be negatively characterized as mannerist, inauthentic, decadent, that emphasizes the conventionality of poetic languages even as it subjects them to refraction and stylization. Its apparent opacities, its hermeticism, are in fact the index of the secret coup that underlies the declarations of commonality of the other tendency as it seeks to "purify the dialectic of the tribe". For the claim to a commonality of language (predicated in any case on the specialization of poetry as a site of language use) and the caustic opacities of poetic modes that challenge representative pretensions are engaged in a continual dialectic long before post-modern theory shatters the dream of a common language with the fragmentary play of language games.

It is perhaps only more evident now that the proliferation of systems of signification – which emerges in time with the division of labour against which the common language of poetry posed itself – militates against the accession of the subject, poetic or otherwise, to singular voice or the establishment of a common language of representation. Under such circumstances, the dissolution of the subject is attended with the failure of representation, a failure which may be pursued with a dedication at once ethical and political.

Healy, a self-confessed mathematician, is placed better than most poets to push this terrain of failure into the preserve of the languages of empirical science, establishing the falterings of the perceptive system itself as the constitutive ground of our missed encounters with the world. In some respects a richly cosmological poetry, this is one that also fractures the textures of the systems that seek to 'colonize' the cosmos. Healy deploys multiple languages and modes of address, poetic and other speech genres, signifying systems in intricate patterns that pursue meaning less in condensation and metaphor (*Dichtung=condensare*) than in dispersal and constellation.

His repertoire ranges from 'an Egyptian method of divination called Ren', through which he subjects the phrase '(The) Republic of Ireland' to anagrammatic permutations which yield such hilarious results as 'her lie-lined tub of crap' or 'life in burlap décor', to acrostics based on 'adenosine triphosphate' or 'cholinesterase', to algorhythmic transformations of the word 'chaos'. Poetry reverts at times to its ground in riddles and the gratuitous pleasures of word-play, the latter yielding such rich *apercus* from the colloquial as:

> hot pants   shirt of fire
> a tart with a heart   a prick of conscience
> – 'Daylight Saving Sex'

Juxtaposition, deconstruction and play are, however, not enjoyed at the expense of an insistent ethical questioning of the closing down of possibilities that the insistence on the 'truth' of any privileged form of signification entails. As the extended syllogisms of syntactically complex logical poems like 'Colonies of Belief' and 'Change & Response' suggest, the refusal of such play and curiosity as Healy's poetry demands risks the atrophy of perceptual and intellectual response in ways that can even be disastrous:

> Because the associative processes
> work so well that the first thing to enter
> their minds seems plausible and because
> centres of impression form by which they
> choose the data which corroborates only
> and because whenever models are shared
> the group concerned protects its own, sealing
> off any disturbing evidence,
> ideas which they think important become
> more and more independent of the world.
> – 'Change & Response'

The risk is not merely hypothetical. In '*Arbor Vitae*', a long poem in three parts which orchestrates perhaps the largest range of modes of signification, languages and semiotic systems, Healy interrogates the tyrannies of an historical instance of 'natural language' regulation, in the form of attempts to force the deaf to articulate: 'Use your voice' becomes a despotic burden that echoes through a poem that mobilizes and constellates an intricate repertoire of sub- and supra-vocal languages. The predicament of the deaf under such a disciplinary regime resonates with linguistic despotisms everywhere while at the same time opening onto the play of multiple possibilities:

> Central doctrines:
> That true language is lingual;
> that one form of expression excludes another;
> that failure is due to lack of effort.

...

> Today,
> fifty years later,
> those still without language at the age of ten
> are classified as being multiply handicapped
> and transferred to a signing unit.
> Ask *them* what it's like to have no native language.
>
> *Use your voice.*
>
> I will get up in the morning.
> I will wash my face and hands.
> I will put my clothes on.
>
> Yes is open, two handed,
> contact of horizontal and vertical.
> No is a small, solitary, upright bird, closing.
>
> Sohac, hasco, shoca.
> – '*Arbor Vitae*'

Healy's human subject is suspended in networks of signification, cosmic, chemical, semiotic, semaphoric, cybernetic:

> Home is an array of data arising out of
> membranes, pressure, chemo- and light sensors
> and, even more so, out of post-sensual processing.
> But I am a fragment of a shadow
> cast by the coherence of energies
> necessary to co-ordinate a colony of six trillion cells.
> – '*Arbor Vitae*'

We find ourselves at moments on the terrain of Beckett, transposed to a post-digital world:

> Each a special case of all or
> each individual a mispronunciation, genealogy
> a prolonged stutter,
> aiming at presence, not

I
I

> All that effort to renovate a vowel.
> – 'Vertices'

The predicament, however, is less that of bringing to presence the stable core of the self, afflicted by temporality and linguistic slippage, than that of 'processing'. The human subject is in a position akin to that of the deaf person obliged to replace 'the auditory nerve, having twenty thousand synapses,/... with a device having twenty two electrodes,/eight of which are functional.' ('*Arbor Vitae*'). This is, to say the least, an epistemological dilemma which, as 'Change & Response' poses it, is radical in its implications for the limitations of social and political group formation:

> Because their senses register only
> zero to five per cent of the world
> and because the short-term memory
> jettisons most of this and because
> the conscious mind is limited
> to seven or eight ideas at one time.....

The figure of the human subject overwhelmed by cosmic power offers the prospects for a sublime poetics. In an earlier tradition, that sublime poetics would have been founded in the confrontation between the rational human subject and the raw force of the natural world and out of that confrontation the superiority of reason and imagination over nature and mortality would be ultimately confirmed. It is the stuff of many a muscular alpine dithyramb. Healy's play with the sublime is altogether more cyborgian and gets, so to speak, deeper under the skin, where the information processing, neural and second level, that is the stuff of human rationality, meets its incapacity:

> Taking that excess of brain energy
> over and above cellular subsistence
> the scale of the subconscious is such
> that it moves in a data space
> ten to the power of twenty b.p.s.
> Which is to say that even should every sense enlarge

> and the smallest gesture overspill with self,
> still transmission, reception,
> is less than one part in a hundred million.
> You might as well try to send the Complete Shakespeare
> by Morse while never getting further than dot
> – 'Envelopes'

The human subject is no sovereign here, is no more than the effect of cybernetic pulses that far exceed conscious grasp:

> My vibrant senses
> my information implosion,
> where do you leave the,
> I don't know, what would you call it,
> the ego, the conscious mind,
> the suburbia of the psyche,
> the just-a-few-words me ticking away
> at a hundred bits per second?
> I might as well take a spoon to a swamp
> while a new one lands in front of me
> every second.
> – 'Envelopes'

The poetic response to this quantum or cybernetic deconstruction of the Newtonian foundations of the phenomenological world rages in *Green 532* from highbrow slapstick – 'how can I avoid slipping through a lattice / that offers no foothold for a human self? / / Am I here at all?' ('Spirals Dance') – to an almost hymnic retrieval of wonder from the precariousness of human existence that has evolved stochastically from the pre-biological soup:

> That man who is about to solve
> the Star crossword with random letters
> took over three billion years to evolve.
> As did I, living matter, sensitive
> To change as fine as that of an electron's orbital,
> a gloria to any maker.
> O vast and subtle congregation,
> the single photon which touches the mind
> is faint as the sound of a drop of water

>   falling a distance of over a thousand miles.
>   Finger brushes against finger in the water,
>   world upon world ready for rising.
>   – 'Envelopes'

The reader's response will vary to taste, in some sense already positioned before the work in a position analogical to that of Healy's human consciousness facing the world. Healy's poetry is unabashedly erudite in sometimes highly specialized ways, often overwhelming the reader with the constellation of 'bits' of information packaged in multiple language games, on occasion careening to the verge of sentimentality, a sentimentality which at times seems a lyrical hedge against an apprehension of the disenchanted cosmos. Given its extensive, paratactic and constellated structures, it demands an attention willing to suspend the desire for crystalline precipitations of incarnated apperception. Its musics are accordingly, Xenakis rather than Webern, looking for analytic equivalents for the complex relations of being rather than expressive condensations of those relations whose ephemerality is often, in fact, Healy's choice material.

If the path of condensation risks a certain arbitrary hermeticism, that of extension risks reversion into a pathos that seems inorganic and compensatory. But it is a risk that repays the attention that the poetry otherwise demands and one which may be the price of opening verse to grounds that are, with substantially ethical and political force, beyond the neatly cultivated purviews of run-of-mill poetry. *Green 532* is an essential volume for our moment.

Notes on Contributors

Michael S. Begnal is a poet, critic and editor of *the burning bush* literary magazine. His collection *Ancestor Worship* is forthcoming from Salmon.

David Butler's awards include The Brendan Kennelly Poetry Competition (2002) and The Ted McNulty Prize (2001). He is currently working on a translation from the Portuguese of Fernando Pessoa.

Louise C. Callaghan's poetry has been widely anthologised, most recently in *The Field Day Anthology of Irish Writing, Volume IV/V: Irish Women's Writings and Traditions*. Her collection of poems, *The Puzzle-Heart*, was published by Salmon in 1999. *Forgotten Light: An Anthology of Memory Poems*, compiled and edited by her, is forthcoming from A&A Farmar.

Ciaran Carson's collection *First Language: Poems* (Gallery, 1993) won the T.S. Eliot Prize in 1993. His translation of Dante's *Inferno* was published by Granta in October.

Nuala Ní Chonchúir won the Cathal Buí Short Story competition in 2001, was nominated for a Hennessy Award for fiction, and was a participant in the Poetry Ireland Introductions readings. Her poetry and fiction is published in *The Sunday Tribune*, *Poetry Ireland Review* and *The SHOp*, among others.

Tony Curtis has published four collections of poetry, the most recent being *Three Songs of Home* (Dedalus, 1998). He edited *As the Poet Said...* – a collection of quotes from Dennis O'Driscoll's 'Pickings & Choosings' column in *Poetry Ireland Review*. A new collection, *What Darkness Covers*, is forthcoming. He is a member of Aosdána.

Alex Davis lectures in English at University College Cork, and is the author of *A Broken Line: Denis Devlin and Irish Poetic Modernism* (University College Dublin Press, 2000), among other titles.

Gerald Dawe has published five collections of poetry, including *The Morning Train* (Gallery, 1999). A new collection, *Lake Geneva*, will be published next year by Gallery. He teaches at Trinity College, Dublin.

Paul Durcan is a previous winner of the Patrick Kavanagh Award, the Irish American Cultural Institute Poetry Award, and The Whitbread Prize for *Daddy, Daddy* (The Blackstaff Press, 1990). His most recent collection is *Cries of an Irish Caveman* (The Harvill Press, 2001).

Ann Egan's poetry is widely anthologised; her first collection, *Landing The Sea*, will appear from Bradshaw Books in 2003.

Diane Fahey is the author of seven poetry collections, including

Metamorphoses (Dangaroo Press, 1988), and *The Sixth Swan* (Five Island Press, 2001).
Celia de Fréine's prizes include the Patrick Kavanagh Award and the Dun Laoghaire Poetry Award (Irish-language). Her collection *Faoi Chabáistí is Ríonacha* won the Duais Aitheantais Ghradam Litríochta Chló Iar-Chonnachta.
Ann Galvin is previously unpublished. A chapbook of her poems will be published by Futhark in 2003.
Yael Globerman is the author of the novel *Shaking the Tree* (1996). She received the ACUM prize for poetry, and the Pais Award for her first collection, *Alibi*.
Paul Grattan's debut collection, *The End of Napoloen's Nose*, was recently published by the *Edinburgh Review*.
T.F. Griffin's first collection, *Cider Days*, was published by Headland in 1990. His *Selected Poems* was published on CD by the Attic Rooms in 1999.
Karen Alkalay-Gut is chair of the Israel Association of Writers in English. She has published numerous collections of poetry, and a biography of Adelaide Crapsey. Her next poetry book, *So Far, So Good*, is forthcoming.
Ah Jian is a poet based in Beijiing.
Fred Johnston's recent publications include the novel *Atalanta* (Collins Press, 2000) and *Being Anywhere – New & Selected Poems* (Lagan Press, 2002). A *Selected Criticism* is due next year.
Heather Jones is a graduate of Trinity College, Dublin and the University of Cambridge, studying history and literature. At present she is researching a Ph.D at Trinity College, Dublin.
Trevor Joyce's *with the first dream of fire they hunt the cold: a body of work 1966-2000* was published in 2001 by New Writers' Press/Shearsman Books.
David Lloyd is Hartley Burr Alexander Chair in the Humanities at Scripps College, Claremont, USA. His critical work includes *Anomalous States: Irish Writing and the Post-Colonial Moment* (Lilliput, 1993), and *Ireland After History* (Cork University Press, 2000). His three collections of poetry are *Taropatch* (Jimmy's House of Knowledge, Oakland, Ca., 1985), *Coupures* (HardPressed Poetry, Dublin, 1987) and *Change of State* (Cusp Books, Berkeley, Ca., 1993).
Tom Mac Intyre is a poet and playwright. His most recent volume of poems is *Stories of the Wandering Moon* (Lilliput, 2000).
Caitlín Maude (1942–1982) was born in Casla in the Connemara

Gaeltacht. Her poetry collections include *Caitlín Maude, Dánta* (Coiscéim, 1984), edited by Ciarán Ó Coigligh; *Caitlín Maude* (Coiscéim, 1988); and *Caitlín Maude: file* (Bari, Italy, edizioni dal sud and Coiscéim, 1985). Her poetry and sean nós singing, for which she was also noted, was issued on record by Gael-Linn in 1975. She was also highly regarded as an actress and dramatist.

Michael Murphy completed an MA in Indian Philosophy and a PhD on Coleridge. He is working on his first collection of poetry.

Maite Díaz Noval, Cuban *Modernista* poet (1864–1936).

Dennis O'Driscoll's recent publications include a selection of reviews and essays, *Troubled Thoughts, Majestic Dreams* (Gallery, 2001) and his sixth collection of poems, *Exemplary Damages* (Anvil, 2002).

Maureen Oliphant is a poet and local historian.

Margaret O'Shea has had poems published in *Cork Literary Review*, *Poetry Ireland Review*, *A Sense of Cork* (Ed. by Patrick Galvin), and *The SHOp*, among others.

Che Qianzi founded with Zhou Yaping and other Nanjing poets the experimental poetry group 'Yuanyang'. His work is included in *Original: Chinese Language-Poetry Group* (translations by Jeff Twitchell), published by Parataxis Editions, 1995.

William Scammell (1939-2000) published nine collections of poetry in his lifetime; his tenth will be published posthumously by Flambard in Spring 2002, and a *Selected Poems* will follow from Peterloo Poets. He won a Cholmondeley Award in 1982, and the National Poetry Competition in 1989. He was a regular contributor of poetry and reviews to the *Independent, London Magazine*, the *Spectator* and *Poetry Review*.

George Seferis (1900–1971) won the Nobel Prize in Literature in 1963.

Gerard Smyth's latest collection is *Daytime Sleeper* (Dedalus, 2002).

Geoffrey Squires's collection *Landscapes and Silences* was published by New Writers' Press in 1996.

Alan Titley, novelist, playwright and scholar, is Head of the Irish Department in St. Patrick's College, Dublin City University.

David Wheatley is a lecturer in English at the University of Hull. His second collection, *Misery Hill*, was published by Gallery in 2000.

Robert Welch is a critic, editor, novelist and poet. He edited *The Oxford Companion to Irish Literature* (Oxford University Press) in 1996. His novels include *The Kilcolman Notebook* (Brandon, 1994) and *Groundwork* (Blackstaff Press, 1997), while among his collections of poetry is *The Blue Formica Table* (Dedalus, 1999). His new novel *The Kings Are Out* is forthcoming.

Maria Ypsilanti is completing a PhD thesis on Ancient Greek poetry at University College, London. Her translation into Greek of a selection of sonnets by Elizabeth Barrett Browning is forthcoming in *Nea Estia*, the Greek literary journal.

Ouyang Yu's most recent publications include translations of Germaine Greer's *The Female Eunuch* and *The Whole Woman* into Chinese.

Books Received

Randolph Healy, *Green 532: Poems 1983–2000*, Salt Publishing.
David Kennedy, *The President of Earth: New and Selected Poems*, Salt Publishing.
Michael Hulse, *Empires and Holy Lands: Poems 1976-2000*, Salt Publishing.
John Matthias, *Working Progress, Working Title*, Salt Publishing.
Jill Jones, *Screens Jets Heaven: New and Selected Poems*, Salt Publishing.
Ed. Christopher Ricks, *Selected Poems of James Henry*, Lilliput Press.
Jeremy Reed, *Heartbreak Hotel: A Tribute to the King in Verse*, Orion.
Michael Standen, *Gifts of Egypt*, Shoestring Press.
Ed. by Speer Morgan, *The Missouri Review*, Vol. XXV, No. 1, 2002.
Robert Alcock, *Time and Tide*, Lesspress.
Niall McGrath, *First World*, Poetry Monthly Press.
Ed. by Talitha Clare & Robin Brooks, *Moonstone 87*.
Gerry Hull, *Historiographilia*.
Ed. by Niall McGrath, *The Black Mountain Review, Issue 6*.
Liz McSkeane, *Snow at the Opera House*, New Island Books.
Ed. by Sebastian Barker, *The London Magazine*, April/ May 2002.
Elsa Corbluth, *The Planet Iceland*, Peterloo Poets.
Ann Drysdale, *Backwork*, Peterloo Poets.
Gary Allen, *Languages*, Flambard/ Black Mountain.
Barry Tebb, *James Simmons R.I.P.*, Sixties Press.
Ed. by John & Hilary Wakeman, *THE SHOp*, Issue 9, 2002.
Patrick Cullinan, *Matrix*, Snailpress.
Ed. by Patrick Galvin, *Southword*, Vol. 3, No.2.
Ed. by Didier Devillez, *Balise 1-2: Politique et Style*, Cahiers de Poétique des Archives & Musée de la Litterature, 2001-2002.
Ed. David Pike, *Pulsar: Poems from Ligden Poetry Society*, September 2002, Edition 3/(02) (31), Ligden Publishers.
Ed. by Françoise Han, *La Traductiere, No. 20: Le bel aujourd'hui / The Waste Land*.
Michael O'Siadhail, *The Gossamer Wall*, Bloodaxe Books.
Jella Lepman, *A Bridge of Children's Books*, The O'Brien Press.
Ann Alexander, *Facing Demons*, Peterloo Poets.
U.A. Fanthorpe, *BC AD: Christmas Poems*, Peterloo Poets.
Anthony Wilson, *Nowhere Better Than This*, Worple Press.
Ed. by Nigel McLoughlin, Matthew Fluharty and Frank Sewell, *breaking the skin: 21st Century Irish Writing (Volume Two: New*

Poetry), The Black Mountain Press.
Mary Branley, *A Foot on the Tide*, Summer Palace Press.
Mary Montague, *Black Wolf on a White Plain*, Summer Palace Press.
Ruth Carr, *There is a House*, Summer Palace Press.
Cevat Çapan, *Where Are You, Susie Petschek* (translated by Michael Hulse & Cevat Çapan), Arc Publications.
Douglas Dunn, *New Selected Poems : 1964–2000*, Faber & Faber.
The Nation's Favourite Poems of Celebrations, BBC Worldwide Ltd.
Ed. by Paul D. Reich, *Sycamore Review*, Volume Fourteen, Number Two.
Ed. by Tim Kendall, *Thumbscrew*, No. 20–21.
Ed. by Oliver Marshall, *Wildeside Literary Magazine*, Issue 4, September 2002.
Lawrence Sail, *The World Returning*, Bloodaxe.
Philip Holmes, *Lighting the Steps*, Anvil Press Poetry.
Sally Purcell, *Collected Poems* (edited by Peter Jay), Anvil Press Poetry.
Knut Ødegård, *Missa* (translated from the Norwegian by Brian McNeil), Dedalus.
Ed. by David H. Lynn, *The Kenyon Review*, Volume XXIV, Numbers 3/4, Summer/Fall 2002.
Ed. by Les Merton, *Poetry Cornwall*, Number Two.
Ed. by Brendan Flynn, *The Clifden Anthology*.
John Ennis, *Near St. Mullins*, Dedalus.
Michael Rosen, *Carrying the Elephant*, Penguin.
Eileen Casey, *Wall Street*, Clothesline Press.
Eamonn McLaughlin, *Poems by Eamonn McLaughlin*, Boudicca Press.
Brenda Williams, *Death and the Maiden and Other Poems*.
Patrick Warner, *all manner of misunderstanding*, Killick Press.
Ed. by Joy Hendry, *Chapman 99*.
John Kennedy, *Flame*.
John McAuliffe, *A Better Life*, Gallery Books.
Razmik Davoyan, *Selected Poems*, MacMillan.
Gabriel Fitzmaurice, *I And The Village*, Marino.
Ed. by Henri Deluy, *Action Poétique*, Numéro 169.
Anna Wigley, *The Bird Hospital*, Gomer.
Katie Donovan, *Day of the Dead*, Bloodaxe.
Ed. by Daniel Veach, *Atlanta Review*, Volume IX, No. 1, Fall/Winter 2002.
Ed. by Niall MacMonagle, *Off the Wall*, Marino.

Carol Rumens, *Hex*, Bloodaxe.
Ed. by David Hamilton, *The Iowa Review*, Volume Thirty-Two, Number Two.
Oscar Van Higham, *Walking On*.
Ed. by Michael S. Begnal, *the burning bush*, No. 8, Autumn 2002.
Ed. by Patricia Oxley, *acumen*, No. 44, September 2002.
Ed. by Pierre Dubrunquez, *poésie*, numéro 93, juin 2002.
Ed. by Pierre Dubrunquez, *poésie*, numéro 94, octobre 2002.
Ed. by Deborah Tall, *Seneca Review*, Vol. XXXII, No. 2, Fall 2002.
Alexander Pushkin, *The Bridegroom* (translated by Antony Wood), Angel Books.
Ed. by David Herd and Robert Potts, *Poetry Review*, Volume 92, No. 2, Summer 2002.
Ed. by David Herd and Robert Potts, *Poetry Review*, Volume 92, No. 3, Autumn 2002.
Ed. by Joy Hendry, *Chapman 100-101*.
Tadhg Gaelach Ó Súilleabháin, *Furnace of Love* (translated by Pádraig J. Daly), The Dedalus Press.
Blair Ewing, *And To The Republic*, Argonne House Press.
W.N. Herbert, *The Big Bumper Book of Troy*, Bloodaxe.
Ed. by David Cobb, *The British Museum Haiku*, The British Museum Press.
Ed. by Robert Minhinnick, **Poetry***wales*, Volume 38, Number 1, Summer 2002.
Robert Fraser, *The Chameleon Poet: A Life of George Barker*, Pimlico.
Ed. by Eddie S. Linden / A.T. Tolley (Guest Editor), *Aquarius 25 /26*.
Ed. by John McNamee, *Out To Lunch*, Bank of Ireland Arts Centre.
Ted Deppe, *Cape Clear: New & Selected Poems*, Salmon.
Dennis O'Driscoll, *Exemplary Damages*, Anvil Press Poetry.
Anne Dean, *Odysseus in the Bathroom*, Bradshaw Books.
Henrik Nordbrandt, *My Life, My Dream* (translated from the Danish by Robin Fulton), Dedalus.
Ed. by John and Hilary Wakeman, *THE SHOp*, No. 10, 2002.
Paul Grattan, *The End of Napoleon's Nose*, Edinburgh Review.

Previous Editors of *Poetry Ireland Review*

John Jordan 1-8	Spring 1981 - Autumn 1983
Thomas McCarthy 9-12	Winter 1983 - Winter 1984
Conleth Ellis & Rita E. Kelly 13	Spring 1985
Terence Brown 14-17	Autumn 1985 - Autumn 1986
Ciarán Cosgrove 18/19	Spring 1987
Dennis O'Driscoll 20-21	Autumn 1987 - Spring 1988
John Ennis & Rory Brennan 22/23	Summer 1988
John Ennis 24-25	Winter 1988 - Spring 1989
Micheal O'Siadhail 26-29	Summer 1989 - Summer 1990
Máire Mhac an tSaoi 30-33	Autumn 1990 - Winter 1991
Peter Denman 34-37	Spring 1992 - Winter 1992
Pat Boran 38	Summer 1993
Seán Ó Cearnaigh 39	Autumn 1993
Pat Boran 40-42	Winter 1993 - Summer 1994
Chris Agee 43/44	Autumn/Winter 1994
Moya Cannon 45-48	Spring 1995 - Winter 1995
Liam Ó Muirthile 49	Spring 1996
Michael Longley 50	Summer 1996
Liam Ó Muirthile 51-52	Autumn 1996 - Spring 1997
Frank Ormsby 53-56	Summer 1997 - Spring 1998
Catherine Phil Mac Carthy 57-60	Summer 1998 - Spring 1999
Mark Roper 61-64	Summer 1999 - Spring 2000
Biddy Jenkinson 65-68	Summer 2000 - Spring 2001
Maurice Harmon 69-72	Summer 2001 - Spring 2002